RAW DEAL

Published by Brolga Publishing Pty Ltd
ABN 46 063 962 443
PO Box 12544
A'Beckett St
Melbourne, VIC, 8006
Australia
email: markzocchi@brolgapublishing.com.au

National Library of Australia Cataloguing-in-Publication data

Raw deal
9781921221910 (pbk.)
McKay, Wayne Phillip, 1977-
Criminals--Australia--Biography.
Ex-convicts--Australia--Biography.
Ex-drug addicts--Australia--Biography.
Sexual abuse victims--Australia--Biography.
Tattoo artists--Australia--Biography.
Musicians--Australia--Biography.

364.1550994

Printed in Singapore
Edited by Evan Joseph and Julie Capaldo
Cover photograph and design by David Khan
Typeset by Imogen Stubbs

RAW DEAL

WAYNE McKAY

CONTENTS

WHOS GOT THE BEATS

I got the beats evolved from the streets
Bringing staunch shit make you jump from your seats
I got my own style walked the dark mile
Real life beats straight off the shit pile
They say Im angry then they call me violent
Put me in the hole try making me silent
My life is my life condemned me to hell
But im back now see with my story to tell.

I talk the talk
And I walk the walk
My soles locked down
Theres a demon to stalk
he tell me rot in hell
Been there done that
Treat me like a dog
Then spin when I attack
Hows that work
Poke sticks you get bit
Lifes on the low people dont give a shit
I am one man one body one mind
But look inside and theres an army you will find
I play it real
Peoples pain I can feel
Got to put it straight
Coz I lived the raw deal

Wayne McKay

INTRODUCTION

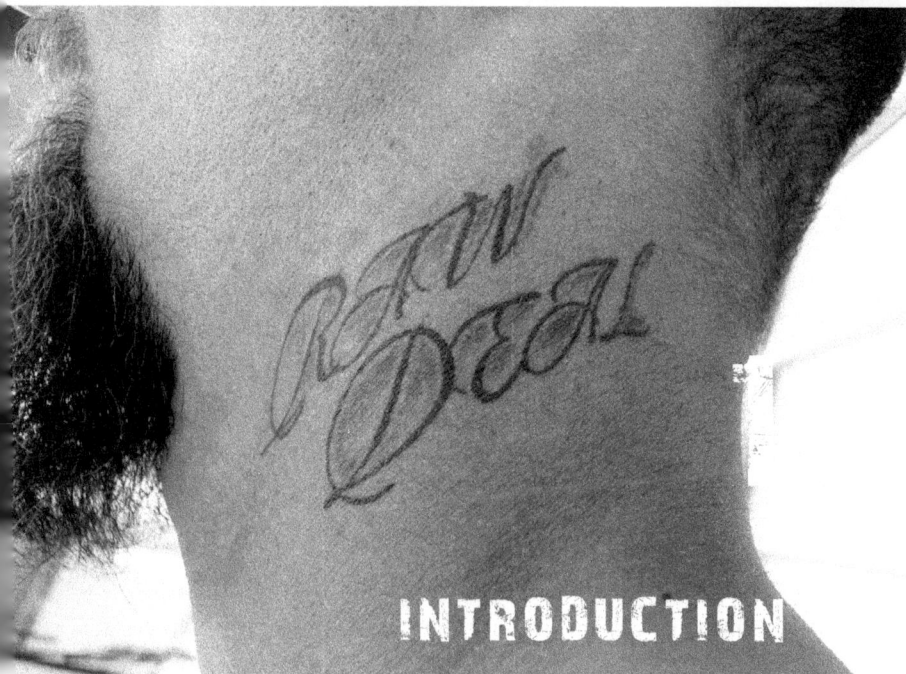

I am a 29-year-old man who has seen a lot. My name is Wayne Phillip McKay, born on the 7-1-77 in Albany regional hospital. I'm an ex-heroin addict, speed addict, pill popper, street criminal, victim of the system. I wrote this book, one: for closure, two: to show people that I was not who they all thought I was, and three: to prove there can be a light at the end of the tunnel. People say that I was crazy. I guess you could say I was, but that was just my way of dealing with the obstacles put in front of me.

Anyone who thinks that I done crime just for the fuck of it you are horribly mistaken. My life did not have any time for fun; I was too busy thinking of ways to hide from my mind and the shit that was in it. I want to send a message to people: don't throw what you can't catch.

I had to fight to get to where I am, and in lots of ways I still have to. Everybody has struggles in their life, I know. I had to fight twelve rounds even to get my brain stable enough to write this book. I rode around on a push-bike, ran and walked to book shops and libraries for two years researching on how to get my story out there. I got a business card from a little bookshop in Swan Hill and took it from there. I took samples of my book to places I thought could point me in the right direction and everyone told me it was really great what I was trying to do, but no one helped me. I did it myself, with the support of my family: my fiancée Michele, my two sons Jayden and Ryley. The birth of my little daughter Tahni pushed me to do something positive.

I don't use real names in this book due to the fact I am not a dog, which in prison terms is a give up, name-dropper, child molester. The word gets thrown around these days like it's nothing but to anyone from the old school that's done any time it's the most putrid word to be put on. I'm no Chopper Reed wannabe. Every state prison has plenty of them. Having been a criminal in the past for many years I have to watch what I say. I don't want to be blamed for any shit I did not do. I am sure there will be a lot of people out there who know me or know of me that will be either shocked to shit that I am still alive or a little pissed off that I am doing well for myself.

I would love to sit here and tell you every little thing I done but due to the drugs and the time some things get a bit blurred. I don't want to seem like a smart-arse, getting off on talking about his crimes. I'm not stupid. I'm not being the easy way out for anyone again. I may have got away with stealing a few cars back then but in the long run I didn't get away with shit. I lived my life looking over my shoulder. I am pretty even with the scores. A lot of people can't seem to understand why someone can be nasty, hate society and have no remorse for the crimes they are committing and have absolutely no respect for authority. Well, I am here to tell you why I went the way I did.

This is not a dig at my parents—this book is about me and why I strayed away from the pack. But I will point out where I felt like I was worthless; when I felt I was not loved. So many of the little things my parents done affected me more than what they could have imagined.

I loved my mother more than anything else in the world. I would draw her pictures and write letters apologising for being a naughty boy and leave them on her pillow so she could find them.

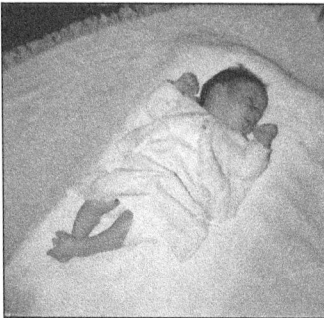

▲ *Baby photo of me looking like a girl, if you ask me.*

▲ *My daughter, Tahni, all cashed up. Who needs a blanket when you got dollar bills.*

▲ *Me with a big smile leaning against my mother's car. I was about 5 years old.*

The next day I would see them in the bin. I hated that. The only way I could get attention was to fuck up. That was the way I lived most of my life. I had no one to love or who loved me. The world was not exactly kind to me. My mother's name was Christine McKay. I had an older brother named Darren and we all lived in a little house on Townsend Street in Mount Lockyer, a suburb of Albany in Western Australia. That's where I grew up and where the memories from this book start.

• • •

My mother, God bless her soul, was a small woman and a hard worker. She worked in the fish factories on Albany's harbour, cleaning all the fish and packing them in freezers. I remember the smell of the fish on her clothes. My aunties or my pop, whoever it was at the time, used to pick her up from work and they'd take me with them. Mum would come out in her white boots with a hair net on her head and a cigarette in her fingers. I can still see the puddles in the bumpy old car park, potholes full of water. People would be running back to their cars. I'd watch the white boots splashing as they ran. I could hear people yelling, "See ya tomorrow! See ya Chris! Yeah see ya!" as Mum took a drag on her cigarette and filled the car with smoke. I remember all that like it was yesterday. Mum would start talking about how shit the day was or how her pay was not right. Back then those things were nothing to me. I didn't understand. All I knew was my mum stank of fish and I couldn't wait to get home and out the car. I was about five.

Mum always kept the house clean and tidy. We didn't have much furniture but Mum done what she could, I guess, with two boys to look after on her own. She always cooked a healthy meal for dinner and things like that. I do have some fun memories, like riding my pushbike into Mum's little Gallant on my seventh birthday. And when we were sitting at my granny's watching tv for the lotto numbers. It was the big jackpot—two million dollars. I was all excited because I heard the whole family talking about all the fancy things they were going to buy with the money when they won. I honestly thought the money was going to be there because they all said they were going to win. I put my order in too, for a new truck, but I never got the truck and none of the family got none of that money either.

Sometimes I'd sit there and watch my granny play the piano. As annoying as it sounded it hypnotised me as well. I'd just sit there and listen. To me, my dear old gran was the greatest woman, standing about five-foot-eight with curly white hair. Big veins used to stick out of her legs, they used to spin me right out. When she wore her bright flower frocks around the kitchen it would always light the whole room up. And the smell of whatever treat she was cooking floating through the air was the best. Always fresh cookies and cakes. She made the best sandwiches. Anytime I was hungry she would prepare the biggest snack for me. The smell of the potbelly fireplace burning in the lounge-room was always a comforting smell. Nice and warm on freezing cold days, which was almost all the time in Albany.

My pop was a grumpy old man always telling me off for whatever he could, but he loved me and for my brother Darren, well, the sun shined out of his arse. I loved my pop, to me he was a hero because he had been in the army. He was a tough old man, always had a roly hanging off his lip and yellow fingers from the way he used to hold his cigarette. He would tell me heaps of old stories. His right hand had something wrong with it that made his hand stay in a position like he was holding a pen. Pop told me it was ran over by a bulldozer when he worked in the railways. I still don't know what really happened to his hand. My pop was a diabetic as well, which I never knew much about. I remember in the fridge there were all his little medicine bottles and my granny would tell me, "Don't you touch that, it will make you sick."

◀ *Me on a motor bike with my Aunty Colleen. I grew to love motorbikes and I think that's where it all started.*

◀ *Me with my brother Darren (Pinkie) sittin' on Santa's lap. I would have been around 7 years old and asking for a motor bike.*

Anything she didn't want me to touch made me sick. Granny's paintings were plastered all over the house. Little paintings of fruit bowls, big paintings of whaling boats, oil paintings in the lounge room of flower arrangements, hobby text cats on the walls. The smell was like mothballs. The whole house had that smell through it.

Mum had six sisters. The oldest was Diane, and Mum was next, then Jeanette, Colleen, Judy and Julianne. I'd always hear one of them being the bitch about something. They had their own problems that I don't really know much about.

My mum and her dad had some issues. I think that was to do with the fact that Mum had me and Darren at such a young age. Mum was fifteen when she had Darren. I'm four years younger. I don't know nothing on that subject so I can't say anything.

I also remember thinking I could fly, because Darren told me I could. See, we had gone to the tip with my pop and after we had scrounged around for a bit we found this great big foam aeroplane. Pop said we could have it, so

▲ *Jayden & Ryley looking the part, ready to go motor bike riding in Swan Hill out bush. Taking after my passion for motor bikes.*

we put it in the trailer and took it home. When we got home we got sick of playing planes with it and my brother had a great idea for me: he snapped both the wings off the plane and sticky-taped them to my arms. Then he helped me to the top of the swing-set and said, "Jump." I did, thinking I could fly, and landed flat on my face, busting my nose. I screamed and ran to my mum, who I think (and hope) kicked Darren's arse.

One of the games I remember playing with Darren when I was about twelve was a game called Knife. In it, we would stand about six feet away from each other, facing one another. We would start with our legs straight and the first person would throw the knife. It was only allowed to land within one foot of your little toe: if it was outside the boundary it was a no-throw. If it was a bad throw it was through your foot. The idea was, wherever the knife landed you had to move your foot, spreading your feet apart. Eventually you were doing the splits and it was like throwing a knife while playing a game of twister. I got one in the big toe a couple of times but that was it; my brother was either a good shot or a jagging prick. I didn't mind playing that game sometimes, it taught me how to throw knives at least. When my brother did get my foot he sucked up big time so he wouldn't get in the shit. If I dobbed we would have both got flogged.

My brother, fine upstanding citizen that he is, I will give him the nickname Pinkie, due to the fact that he cut his little finger off to show his mates how much of a hero he was. He then told everybody some bullshit story he dropped a barbeque plate on it. The truth of the whole situation was that I bought him this Samurai sword during a two-month period when I liked him. My brother went and rounded up a few of his little sheep mates and went to the car park at the Yangebup Primary School. He sculled a little bottle of Jim Beam, and then, as you do, pulled his shiny new sword out of his car, put his finger on the curb and cut it off. After that one Russell and all the rest of my brother's toy-boys drove to the hospital and made up some bullshit story.

On that note I'd just like to say a big *Howdy* to me old mate Pinkie. One night when I was about fifteen he was told I was going to steal the new motorcycle he had just bought. It was a ZXR Kawasaki, and it was a really nice-looking bike, and that's all I said to my mother. But somewhere between me saying that to her and her talking to him it was put across that I had said I was going to pinch his bike. I only visited my mother that day and in conversation said, "That's a wicked bike." Anyway, my brother hunted me down. I was at a park in Southlakes, just at the back of the shopping centre, sitting on the swings. Me and my mate Robert and Kylie, a friend from my school who I hadn't seen since I left home, and another girl Cassandra were sitting there, just laughing and messing around. Then Pinkie showed up in a banged-out old van. I had no idea what was going on but as soon as the sliding side door of the van opened I knew something wasn't right. You don't bring seven people to say *G'day*. My brother walked straight for me. As his steps got faster my heart beat faster. I didn't expect what happened next: he leant down, grabbed a handful of sand and threw it straight in my eyes and mouth. As soon as my eyes shut all I felt was punches all over my head and face. I pulled my hands in to cover my face but one of his friends pulled my hands away so they could get a clean shot.

Spitting sand I screamed, "You dog cunt! Weak cunts! Mobbing dogs!" How tough was he? Him and his mates had been doing martial arts for at least four years. I had never done a day in my life. What hurt the most about that day was I wet my pants because my brother put me in a sleeper hold and I blacked out. I was left in that park bleeding. From that day on I hated him and Mum because I honestly had thoughts in my head that Mum was just trying to get me hurt.

Another time I was invited to his twenty-first birthday party. At that stage in my life I was living in Yangebup with the local baker and his wife. Mum just lived up the road and was holding the party at her house because my brother was living back at home. Anyway I made this birthday cake at work for him. It was of a great big cat with a doughnut for the ass. I made it that way because

I thought my brother needed some pussy in his life. I thought it would be a good laugh but unfortunately for me it was not seen like that because Mum put a condom on the candle and I got the blame. My brother got drunk and smashed me in front of the whole party. He walked straight up and head-butted me, knocking me clean out. But that wasn't enough. I came around in just enough time to feel him kicking the shit out of me while I was on the ground. Then he grabbed me by the back of my hair and smashed my head into the toe-ball of his van. All my parents did was stand there and when they'd all seen enough my step-dad came and pulled him off me. My entire family saw it, but no-one done nothing. My little brother and sister seen the whole thing. I ended up in hospital and I still wear the scars from it today.

•   •   •

My mother had met this bloke by the name of Peter. Fine lad, he was a typical Aussie and swept me mum off her feet. I don't know where she met him, all I know is he lived in Perth and we lived in Albany. To me, he was really cool when he visited. He used to take me to the shops and buy me lollies and take me cruising in his car. It wasn't long until we all moved to Perth to be one big happy family.

The first house we moved to was in north Fremantle. It wasn't a bad house, it just stunk of rats that used to live in the old boxes in the shed. I think I was about 7 years old then.

I really looked up to Peter. He worked hard as a mechanic and was really handy with his hands. He could fix anything and he built some mad speedway cars. He used to race every Sunday. Those were the days: we'd get up early and Peter and his mates would have the trailers loaded. We'd go off to the Bibra Lake speedway—plenty of beer for after the race. The smell of the speedway was my favourite smell; I loved the fumes. All I ever wanted to do was be like my step-dad, he was my hero. Speedway lunch was pies with sauce and a can of Coke. I loved that. Me and my brother and whatever other kids were there used to climb up to the highest point we could to watch the races. The old watchtower was our favourite place, but we'd get in the shit for going up there if we got caught. I can't remember who Peter used to race with, but they were both good at it. Peter raced super Sedans and stock cars, as well as doing smash up derbies.

Peter worked hard to build up his own spray-painting panel beating and mechanics business. We then moved, as a family, to Hamilton Hill—just up the road from where Peter's workshop was. The house was older than the house in Fremantle but it was cool. That was the house where I first learned I could draw what I saw. Peter worked hard to bring home nice things for us: he bought us an above ground pool, which was great to splash around in after school. Mum had my little brother Scott in that house, and that was a big change in our life. I loved little Scott and I still do. After he was born, my stepfather asked me and Darren to call him Dad. I didn't want to but my brother did. I think the reason I didn't want to was because I knew I had a different dad somewhere and I didn't really understand, but still we called him Dad and it was alright.

At that time I was going to Hilton Primary and I'll be honest: I was getting in a bit of shit at school for not listening and for being loud in class. The kids I hung around with were just like me—if not worse. I had a little girlfriend who used to always share her chips with me. We were both about eight years old. The little girl's name was Pia. She was my best mate back then. I seen her once again when I had left home. She had grown into a pretty teenager by then and had a boyfriend and a job. I was still doing crime.

When I was going to that school the headmaster's name was Mr Shoesmith. He had a bit of a problem with my brother in the past and that did not seem to go in my favour. The cuts were in at that time as well. Some call it the cane; we called it the cuts. I think I got the cuts twice for being a shit head.

I remember that school well because I had a really good classmate. His name was Scott, same as my little brother. He was my first real buddy that I can remember. We were all ways hanging out at school and causing trouble together in the classroom. Our favourite game was a game we called Push-Offs, where we all stood on the old tractor tyres in the schoolyard and the last one standing on the tyres won. I remember being there one day and all of a sudden the teachers came and pulled me and David, our other mate, aside to tell us Scott had been run over by a car. The car had been on the back of a tow truck and Scott had been riding his pushbike.

That was my first experience with death and it really messed me up. Rest in peace, brother.

School was never the same for me after that. Scott's death had a big effect on the whole school. The school had a memorial for him and a few people got up and said prayers for him. I think the thing that made me deal with it was at my house: Dad had a super Sedan he just bought and was going to race. I used to sit out the back in it and pretend I was racing and doing pit changes. Scott was my imaginary co-driver. I had seen this movie *Six Pack* starring Kenny Rogers and six little kids that used to go to the race days and fix Kenny's car. Kenny Rogers reminded me of my stepfather a bit. That was my favourite movie (that and *BMX Bandits*).

After living in that house for a few years, Dad bought our first house, which was in Yangebup on Dotterel Way. Yangebup's streets were named after birds; it was a new area being built up. Our house was a really horrible-looking place when we first moved there, but it became a beautiful house. The people that were living in it before us were really messy: the lawn hadn't been mown at all—I think since the house was built. The place was not old. The people that lived there just did not care about the house. There was a big skeleton there when we went to inspect the house the first time. It was sitting in the lounge room with a top hat on.

The house became pretty cool when we all worked our arses off cleaning it up. The train-line ran straight past the backyard. I loved it. I used to stand there and count all the carriages and when no one was looking I'd pelt rocks at them. This was around the time my sister, Janice, was born. She was a little darling. I remember pushing her around on a little plastic bike; I done all the race noises and she loved it. Janice and Scott were funny little ones as well. Two little soldiers they were, and they both looked like Peter. Because we'd moved I was going to the Yangebup Primary School, which I hated. I couldn't make any real friends. The kids called me *Fangs* because I had buckteeth, and *Flapper*, because of my big ears. This one kid Shannon Long used to punch me in the ears. I fucken hated that kid and that school. I'd go to school thinking: *This is it. Today I'm going to get him,* but every time I even got close to him he smacked me one and man did it sting. I used to steal his lunch out of the lunch basket after that, and boy did it taste good! He always ordered a chicken schnitzel-burger and I always ate a chicken schnitzel-burger. The canteen ladies didn't know what was going on. Well, at least I think they didn't, but I was doing it for ages. Maybe they cottoned onto it and just didn't let me know. Either way, they stopped me doing the lunch-orders.

I stole the teachers stickers and got caught because I was sticking the stickers on my work and taking it home saying I earned it. But I told my brother and my brother dobbed on me, which did not help me out at all. I got in a lot of shit over that: grounded for a month. Not that it mattered anyway. I was never allowed out: only as far as our front lawn. When we got that house in good nick we sold it and Dad bought a bigger, better house. I was about twelve when I moved there. This was the house where my life changed forever.

The house was still in Yangebup but in a little court. A nice and quiet street. Well, it seemed that way. Dad had been married previously to a lady, who I don't think I ever met. It was around the time she died of cancer that things all changed. I remember Mum was always at the old man: *Where had he been? Who had he been with?* Some nights plates used to go flying across the kitchen. There would be food all over the place. Mum would be screaming while she was drinking wine from the cask in the fridge. Fruitilexia: it was my mum's favourite back then, that and Ouzo. One day I come home from school to find Mum OD-ing on pills, whatever she could get her hands on, I'm not too sure what they were. Mum would be on the phone telling people she loved them and saying her goodbyes with tears in her eyes. Mum waiting to die. Talking to me through a locked sliding door telling me to fuck off. I started crying and screaming at her to stop it and let me in. I was screaming at her, "I love you, Mum." She just screamed at me and told me to go away. I went looking for something to throw through the door and Dad walked around the corner, fucking pissed.

He said to Darren, "Get the kids out of here before I kill your mother."

Darren looked at him in the eyes and said, "You do that and I'll kill you."

Dad just ignored him and went inside to Mum.

Dad would drive home from work in Hilton to

Yangebup, about 10 minutes away, to see what she was trying to do. He'd lose it but take her to the hospital. I'd get the blame for the mood Mum was in, too. Mum thought Dad was having an affair. Any female driving around on their own was suspect; we would follow cars around for hours and Mum would make me write down numberplates, thinking Dad was fucking whoever was driving the car. The people had no idea we were following them, at least I think they didn't. Sometimes we would follow them from one end of town to the other. If Dad was working late we drove past his work to see what cars were parked at the front of the workshop. Mum would flip out if she recognised any cars, and accuse Dad of having girls at his work. Dad always claimed his innocence. Sometimes they fought all night, banging doors, yelling off the top of their lungs at each other. Mum would wake us up and tell us we were going back to Albany. In the middle of the night we would pack the car and start driving. We never got any further than Armadale, and Mum would turn around and drive home or to a friend's house. Dad would either ring Mum, or Mum would ring Dad. They would sort it out and then they'd be into it again the next day or so. We were lucky enough to get two days break every now and then. My schoolwork was going downhill, not that it was much good anyway, but I was getting worse. My grades in my school report were Cs, Ds, and Fs, due to all the troubles at home.

I was not allowed to go out and play with the kids from school. I was always in trouble with my parents.

I used to think my mum exaggerated things to get me in trouble. I had to fold the clothes, do the dishes, sweep the pergola, feed the cat, clean the car, do the gardens. I think Mum got real frustrated with me. I honestly thought Mum hated my guts. When her and Dad weren't fighting then I was in the shit. When they were fighting I would soon be in the shit, when they stopped fighting. I loved them both. Sometimes when they would fight I'd get in between and make shit a whole lot worse, because I would feel like I had to choose a side. I hated that shit, but it wasn't long before I hated them both. Whenever I would get in trouble I'd just go do my chores and I know all children should do chores but there should also be some kind of a reward. Well, not for me. Pinkie was allowed to go out and play with his mates. I wasn't. At that time I was twelve years old, nearly thirteen. He was sixteen, going on seventeen. He was my idol; everything he done, I admired. He was a good fighter and he smoked; he done all the things I thought cool dudes done. Pinkie never really had time for me because he too was trying to get free from the madhouse we were living in, so I was stuck there on my own.

I won't bullshit you and say my life had no fun times, because I'm sure it did. I just don't remember them all. I won't sit here and slag my parents off because I have done plenty of that in the past. Let's just say that from a very young age I honestly felt that I was not wanted.

I remember starting BMX racing at the Hamilton Hill BMX track. My first race meeting I rode to the track—all the way from Yangebup to Hilton. I paid my five dollars and the race coordinators gave me a little green number plate for my handle bars. I put it on and was ready to race. The day's event was called the West Coast Classics. The world champion was in my race. Believe it or not, I beat him! He crashed his bike over a jump and I went on to come first. I won a trophy for the first time in my life. I rode all the way home, on top of the world, all excited with my good news. But when I got home no one gave a shit. To be honest, they didn't believe I even won the trophy. I went on to win another one at a different race meeting. I still didn't get any praise, but I stuck it in their faces. *I did win!* I smashed the trophies in a fit, though, and I never won another one. I only raced there twice, and I came home with a trophy both times. Why didn't they say "Good on ya?" That affected me in a big way. I was shattered when no one really gave a shit that I done well in something.

There were about nine kids living in the street and to the passer-by everything would seem normal, but it wasn't. Long before we moved to that street the kids were involved in sexual behaviour. The people that lived in our house before us had teenage kids and they too were involved. I'm not pointing fingers just stating facts. The shit these kids were doing was not that *show-me-yours-I'll-show-you-mine* stuff: it was more than that. I was involved too, but I had no idea what sex was. My parents kept the sex talk out of our little heads, so it was all new to me. The one that introduced me to it was Dean. We'd all go down the bush and play in the bushes.

19

This all went on for about six months until the boys next door got caught doing something with their little sister, and whatever it was landed me right in the shit. They all blamed whatever happened on me. They said *I* taught them whatever it was they were doing and *I* was accused of doing something to little Chloe.

Now I have lived my whole life rotting inside for something I never done. I admitted to everything I done but I was not copping that shit. Mum tells me she went and stood up for me and nearly smashed the mother. But I never saw that, I was too busy at home getting the fuck ripped out of me. I was looked at like a disgusting dirty piece of shit, guilty till found innocent. *I was a victim.* They all blamed me, saying I was the teacher of all the dirty shit they knew.

Now I am an adult, my mum tells me that the adults were having sex parties. I never seen none of that shit: it didn't go on in our house. No one ever told me none of that shit back then. Everyone was innocent except me. All the parents in the street made sure the finger was pointed at me. I already had troubles at home with Mum and Dad fighting all the time. I don't know what happened to the other kids but no one else ever admitted to anything. I admitted to shit they didn't even know about. I lived a very sheltered life in the way of sex. I had no friends to hang out with and talk the shit kids talk, so I didn't know what head-jobs or wank-offs were. I was the school loser. All I knew about anything sexual was I was a *cock, head-fuck stick* and a *pussy* when I walked away from confrontation. I learnt what I knew in that street.

They tried to have me charged for sexually assaulting the little girl but they pulled out. Honestly, my beliefs are that something was going on and I was the easy way out. I have paid for it my whole life. Mum and Dad started getting stuck into me after that. I went to school with bruises all up my back and my arse. I fucken hated everyone: my teachers, my parents, my brother, all except little Scottie and little Janice. I went to school one day and I had bruises all over me, on my dick, up my back, down my legs, all over my arse; great thick welts. My dick looked like a big purple blood blister. The belt flicked around and whacked me. I was in some fucked up pain that night, I pissed all over the floor while I was getting belted.

When I went to school I got in trouble and they said they were going to call my parents. I lost the plot and said, "Do it! I don't give a fuck you don't know nothing about me. Every time you send letters home this is what happens to me." I pulled my pants down right in front of half the school and ripped my t-shirt off. The teachers panicked and covered me up quickly. They took me to the office. From there they started sucking up my arse, being all nice to me. They rang the Fremantle Welfare Department who then came to the school and picked me up.

They took me to the Fremantle office and talked to me. I told them what had happened at home. They took photos of me and documented everything. Mum was called down to the Fremantle office to see what was

21

going on and when she got there I was in a little room waiting. She walked in the room with a look on her face like she had no idea what all this was about. That look sent me into a rage.

She said, "You brought it on yourself, Wayne."

I lost it at her and said, "You will pay for this, Mum. I fucking hate you and Peter," and the workers grabbed me and took me out of the room. I didn't see Mum again for two weeks. I was nervous as hell. I didn't know what was about to happen. I didn't want my parents to get in trouble but I also didn't want to get another belting. I had had plenty of them over the past twelve months.

I was put into a foster home for about two weeks. My foster parents were very nice people. Their names were Frank and Lisa. Lisa was a little lady with black hair and gentle features, standing about five foot four, and Frank was not much taller. He had short brown hair and an American accent. He was also my introduction to American rap on vinyl. Their house was in Willagee. It was a lot older than Mum and Dad's house, but it had a nice feel to it. Willagee was known to be a real rough area at the time: heaps of crime. And the Burnie murders. But their house was fine. While I was there no one ever broke in. Frank delivered chemicals all over Perth and I used to go to work with him on the Saturday. I loved cruising around in the truck. Frank and Lisa were very nice people who could not have kids, that's why they fostered kids. They wanted to adopt and they were on the list or something. They really loved me, well, it sure felt like they did. I have nothing against them. I wished my parents were more like them.

I went to school at Southlakes High. I was in year eight. They made my lunch every day and made sure I always got to school okay. It was all going good for me until a lady from the Fremantle Welfare Office came and told my foster parents that they had to make a choice to let me go or they would not be allowed to foster another child again, and they could very likely lose my little foster brother Scott. The reason for this was because I was involved in sexual activity in my street, but what these low life assholes didn't actually know was that I was a victim. Those kids were a lot more mature about what was going on than I was, and nobody, not even my parents, believed me. My life at home was destroyed from all that shit and now so was my new life. This is just a message to the adults that lived in my street and condemned me to a life of shit, you dirty rotten pieces of shit, yes, I still remember everything. You should really look inside yourselves now and find what really happened. I was no sick kid. I done what I was taught, playing what the other kids played. I didn't go through life preying on kids. The thought of it makes me sick. I still feel ill from the part I played in all that shit. Why did my life go the way it did? I'd love to see how the other families pulled out of it. I was grounded and had my arse kicked every time I breathed. I went to school with welts all up my back and all over my arse. Ryan, Dean and the others were all still out in the street playing the next day, giving me dirty looks. I don't blame them anymore. I blame the parents. As far as I am concerned those kids were once victims, too. The parents know who they are and what they done but that's cool, because I firmly believe you get what you dish out. I did. In this life or the next, you get what you dish. I know when you are twelve, thirteen, you know what's right or wrong. And if I done wrong I got dealt with. My whole life I could never have sex without feeling dirty. I really can't handle people touching me in an affectionate way. I get paranoid about whoever is sitting next to me; if their foot touches mine I feel uncomfortable thinking I am sending off some signal that I want to be touched. I hated everyone when the welfare made me feel like I was a dirty child, all they done was got involved and left me for dead. No one but them motherfuckers in that street knew who was really the teachers of all that shit. I've questioned myself, blamed myself, doubted myself, and I'm done with it. There was nothing wrong with me except what was programmed into me: *hate*. I understand that they had to think about others but all they had to do was talk to me, to see what was going on. No one listened to me and that, my readers, is where a boy turns.

I was returned home. That lasted a week. My parents were dirty on me because I basically dobbed on them. I felt like they all wanted me dead. It seemed like it was an effort for anyone to talk to me. One day when I came home from school. I asked if I could do something, and Mum said, "No, you can fold the clothes."

So I said, "You act like a witch to me."

My mum lost it and said, "You wait till your father gets home! Get in your room! Call me a bitch!"

I said, "I called you a witch, not a bitch." But it was too late. Mum rang Dad and he flew home from work with the devil in his stride. I was going to get it. I heard the front door open and shut.

"Where is he?" a voice yelled.

"In his room," Mum said.

I was shitting myself.

He came to my room and said, "Come with me."

Something looked different about the way he was handling the situation.

"Come on out here," he said.

I followed saying, "What are you going to do? I didn't call you a bitch, Mum, you know I didn't."

"Yes you did, Wayne, yes you did," said Mum.

Dad said, "Follow me" as he walked to the big shed out the back. I was crying and shaking. Mum stayed in the house at the door, and I heard it slide shut behind me. I was nervous as hell. We got to Dad's shed and he still hadn't said nothing. He unlocked the door and opened it. The beach buggy was in the middle of the shed. I walked in and *thump!* in the back of the head. I was launched forward and almost fell over. I panicked and ran forward around the buggy. Dad pulled the door shut behind him, ever so calmly, and walked up the other side of the buggy. He had hate in his eyes, and I didn't know what the fuck to do when he picked up the hacksaw out of the toolbox. Then he started saying, "I'm gonna teach you. I'm gonna teach you." He was getting louder as he was walking towards me.

I lost it and found balls from nowhere.

I said, "You can all get fucked!" I ran at the door and booted it. I slid it open and ran up the driveway. He chased me a little bit and then stopped. I got to the top of the driveway turned around and said, "You wait. I'll get you. I am going to fucken get all of you. Fuck you." Then I took off. Dad was yelling something as I ran down the street. All the kids were out the front playing. I was crying and yelled at them all, "Thanks a lot, fucken liars." All of their heads dropped to the ground and that was the last I ever saw of them kids.

I went and seen my friend Daniel's mum in Southlakes. Her name was Kerrie. A tiny little women compared to my height at that age. Her hair was curly like sheep's wool and she was a very fit and healthy woman. She had always been really nice to me. She took me to the welfare office because I couldn't stay with her; they were having problems with Daniel and his step dad. Daniel was a kid from high school. Only thing was, he never went to school. He had his own problems going on at home. I only ever got to see him on my way home from school. He'd be hanging out down the park with the local kids that didn't go to school. I was feeling like shit because I didn't know what my father was going to do with that hacksaw back in the shed. *Was he going to kill me? Or cut something off me?* Mum acted like she hated my guts. My brother Darren didn't talk to me and my little brother and sister were too young to know what was going on. I hated myself.

▲ Artwork

One of my lead pencil drawings. I call it "my life story". There are many different parts to it. The coin slot in the centre represents my mother who couldn't get a refund on me. The hand with the mouth and eyeball is my image of the prison officers and anyone of authority yap yapping in my ear, as well as me hearing voices. The alien baby foetus is me and relates to my mother dropping something. The distorted screaming face is me angry, while the zippers and stitches are all in the same meaning as the bars. They tell of how I felt constricted, as I have been most of my life—mentally and physically. The piano keys down the bottom right hand corner are my keys to a happier life. It's a picture representing feelings of being mixed up, confused and angry but with a light at the end of the tunnel.

HEY MAH

Mother I know you were lost
You had to stick to the light
You didnt want to loose
That man by your side
I forgive you now mum
The past days are fading
Ive found love in my life
This brother aint hating
Im different now
My mind is now grown
Im the strongest youve seen
Coz I grew on my own
Life threw some bricks
That shatterd my teeth
But I swim still mah
To the top of that reef
Each day I live
I live with a smile
The pains still within
That dark dusty mile
But watch my strength shine
My heart beats just fine
Answerthephoneitsmeontheline

Its been years and tears
Nightmares and fears
Voice to the wind
Hope somebody hears
I was everything I was

Been all ive been
But didnt you know
It was me in this thing
You knew me as a baby
Bundle of fun
Iknowdeepthatyoulovedmeoncemum

I will tell you the truth
And hope you will listen
I hated you once
But something was missing
I wished I would die
To see if you would cry
I needed you once
Mum I cant deny
I was near at times that
You didnt even know
I had tears in my eyes
But they had to go
An animal I was
Fed from the bins
Maybe I will burn in hell for all of my sins
Live or die
You wont see me cry
Ive seen my share
Id enjoy the fry
My skins already melted off
Ive drank the poison to make me throff

Wayne McKay

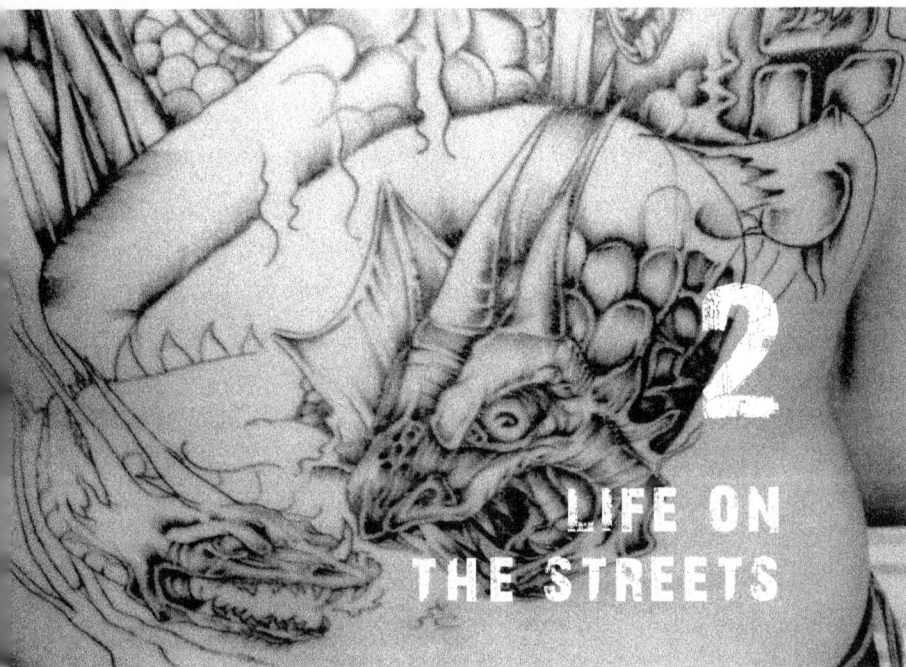

2

LIFE ON THE STREETS

I was put into the Bedford Hostel in Perth city. I was fourteen. I thought I knew everything but I didn't know shit from clay. The other youths in the hostel had experienced the hard life. I thought I had. But I hadn't even touched the surface. They looked miserable, angry and lost, talking to each other like shit, stealing things off each other, sniffing glue, telling the group workers to fuck off when they were asked to do chores. There were names and initials engraved everywhere from the kids that had lived in the place: little messages like *jarad davies is a dog*. Big thick black texta marks throwing up gang tags: CBS – *Can't Be Stopped*; SK – *Siko Killas. Toonie, Freo Boys,* and a great big *Fuck You*: the shit was written on everything, in the toilets, on the phone, on the tv, up the top of the basketball ring.

The place smelt like shit. It smelt stale and the food we got there was mostly the left overs from the lunch vans that cruised around the factories the day before. Everything was dirty with handprints. No one cleaned up after themselves. It was a big change from my nice clean house and the foster house I had stayed in. This was a big wake up call. My life was about to change dramatically. I was fresh to the street and raw to the beat.

It was not long before I started sniffing glue and Torlene to fit in. All the other kids done it and I was not about to become the odd one out in a pack of hawks and be called the weak cunt. It was hard for me to fit in because I didn't know nothing about street life. I didn't know none of the lingo, my clothes were dorky ones that the welfare had got for me from my home. I had to do something to fit in with them so I just went along and did what they did. We went for a walk during the day, me and two other kids: Donna and another little kid. He was her bitch, and she called him that. She made him do all the shoplifting. When we got to the Claremont hardware store he stole the quick grip. I was nervous at first, wondering what it was going to do to me. I watched how the other kids done it and copied and that shit was worse than the glue because it burnt all my throat. But it wasn't like sniffing through your nose it was more inhaling the fumes through your mouth.

That shit fucks you right up: hearing a constant *zing-zing-zing* noise in the background, walking around the city in a coma. Lights are on but nobody's home. Swearing at people trying to start trouble when I could barely stand straight. I thought I was hardcore because I sniffed that shit with the other kids, acted out as something I was not, spilling glue all over my clothes. I'd stash the glue bag up the sleeve of my jumper so it just looked like I had my hand up to my mouth. The taste hits the back of your throat and everything goes numb. It's hard to explain what it done, or to describe what I seen, but it was like a fairy tale, like *The Wizard of Oz*, only it was all black and white, black and white spinning wheels. I saw the moon. At least, I thought everything made sense to me like I understood all the bizarre things in my mind. When I came back around I got a headache and realised that the horrible fucked place was still there, and so the best thing was: if you didn't want a headache, keep sniffing. When I was off the planet, on the glue or the petrol, I would have been comfortable enough to just go to sleep and not wake up. When I was straight I'd think about things way too much, play every part of my past over and over in my head. I lost touch with any real nice memories I had so I chose to stay off my face. People would see me on the train and say things to me like: *Get off the train! How old are you? Where are your parents?* They would even tell me they were going to take me to the train conductor. Once some big fat bogan lady smashed my glue-bag into my face. I started blacking out on the train with the bag up to my mouth. At the time I didn't see the good in it at all; I lost it at her and flung the bag at her and jumped off the train when it stopped. I had glue all over my face for weeks after that, picking little bits off all the time. Usually, I'd

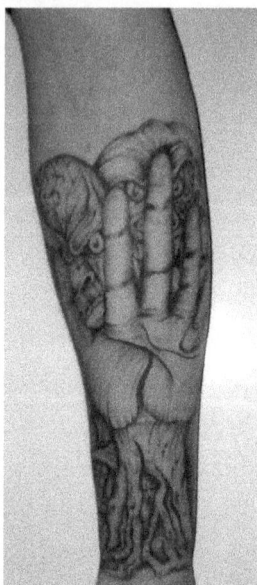

Forearm tattoos

◀ *This is a tattoo I done on a good friend of mine, Craig. I taught him how to tattoo and he swapped all his music equipment with me. It was a freehand tattoo done in a black and grey wash.*

▶ *Craig's arm. It's one tattoo that goes all around his arm. Freehand twisted design, a mixture between mine and Craig's design. Done in Swan Hill 2006.*

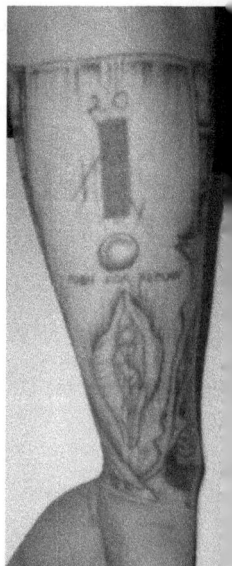

laugh at them all, like: Who the fuck are you to pry into my business? The glue-bag would stink the whole train carriage out, but I couldn't smell a thing. It was like my life support. Only thing was, you eventually got kicked out of all the hardware stores because they knew what you were up to—the glue stock was going down daily. When you couldn't get it on the odd day you got the headache from hell.

I started sniffing with Donna. She was a big butch girl with red hair and bodgy tattoos done in blue Indian ink all over. She was the scariest person I knew back then. She done shit to me that I won't talk about in too much detail because that is shit I leave where it lies. But she wasn't no ordinary sixteen year old girl. She had been raped, stabbed, and bashed many times. She smashed on like a bloke. I heard her screaming at someone one night:

Do you know what it's like to have a beer-bottle shoved up yah? Huh, dog? Do yah? Don't tell me you know what I'm feeling! I'll shove a bottle up your hole and see if you like it. She was evil this girl: she liked you one minute and the next was telling you: *You're a dog!* and *I'm going to kill you, cut your throat and stick your dick in your arse!* I couldn't handle it.

The group workers didn't do shit, they were just people who could not get a job so they thought they liked kids and could help them. But after a while they all turned the same, just turn the other cheek and go home at night. Some of them were nice, usually because like me they were fresh and didn't know the rules. The Welfare should have told me what to expect in the place. Once Welfare dropped me off I didn't see them again while I was at the hostel. After that, I think I may have had appointments once or twice to see a counsellor, but I never went. I'd rather go and hang around the city. I hadn't been there too many times at all when I lived at home. In fact, I think I may have been there only once, and that was just sitting in the car with my mum.

The police were always coming and going from the hostel because of the kids who stayed there who were out doing crime and causing trouble. I'd spin out because the kids there didn't give a fuck. They told the police to all go get fucked, calling them dogs as soon as they pulled into the driveway and spitting on their cars. I thought the police were something you feared if you were a kid. People like my parents would say, "The police will get involved and you don't want that."

If you waved to a copper or asked why they get called dogs and shit then you'd look like a dickhead. How do I know that? Because I made the mistake of saying *hello* to one of them and I got hell for it. I didn't make that mistake again. There were no rules in the hostel: the rules changed with the workers.

I started sleeping on the streets to get away from the hostel. Nothing ever got done because nothing was ever said. I was embarrassed by the whole thing. Donna was known for stabbing people. She had a boyfriend once who killed someone. To me back then that shit was scary. I hadn't met no one like that. Her and her friends hated me. The reason for this was that I fucked up once, saying to her to leave me alone or I was going to tell the group workers. After that I was a *dog*. I didn't know what dog meant back then but I soon learnt. It was a person who dobs. She terrorised me to the point where I stayed away from the hostel as much as I could. But she also found me easily on the streets when I least expected it.

I'd walk around for hours looking for someone to talk to in early hours of the morning. I used to see the street-sweepers cruising around the mall on their little machines. I'd sit in the centre of the mall on one of the chairs and look around in the shop windows, security guards walking up and down the front of the shops about every three hours. Some nights I'd stay awake all night until daylight and then the next day would drag along slow as ever. I'd be that tired sometimes I'd walk and nod off to sleep while I was walking.

I was scared of the streets. I'd never even been outside

my house after seven at night unless I was with my Mum
and Dad. I'd get scared putting the rubbish out the front
on bin nights and I'd run to the front door if I heard a
noise. That's how frightened I was of the dark time. I was
a little wimp. At times it didn't seem real to me because
I could remember my home so well: my family was just
there. Only a couple of months ago I had a Mum that
loved me. Once I had a Dad that took me to work with
him on the weekends. I had a push-bike and a pet cat
called Stubbie I slept in pyjamas. Eight o'clock bedtime.
My life before all the trouble was normal. Sure I got
in trouble but my life was as normal as any one else's
and then I moved to here for my new home: hell, in a
city hiding from shadows and people that didn't like me.
They had a lot of experiences with hate. I had a lot to
learn and that fat bitch was going to teach me.

I was asleep in a toilet block across the road from the
Perth City Mission hostel. I didn't want to stay there because I had heard heaps about it at the last hostel I stayed
at. And, also, I really had no idea what the fuck I was
doing. I woke up that night with a sprinkle on my head.
I felt the warm liquid running down my face. Shock.
It tasted salty. I instantly spat it away from my mouth. I
looked up and they were all laughing at me. I was being
pissed on by some dirty cunt called Chris. I only knew
his name because Donna said, "Kick the cunt out of him,
Chris." He had a tattoo of a cross near his right eye. He
punched me all around the face, calling me a little dog,
booting me in the guts. I just cried and moaned, rolled
up into a little ball. I gave them something to do, I sup-

35

pose. Man, they hated someone, and I got that person's serving of anger. They left me there, bleeding and took off laughing.

I was getting electric shocks of anger through my body. I screamed, "I fucking hate you, Mum!" I just lay there till daytime. Nothing else could have topped what just happened. I felt dirty. I just wanted to die. I hated my life. I hated those cunts. All of it was just creating a demon in me.

I got some new clothes from a Salvo bin in the city: a green jumper that didn't even cover the full length of my arms. They were second-hand, but they were better than smelling like piss. I washed my head at the drinking fountain in the park because the taps in the toilet had no handles. I hated myself more and more each day. Why did I hate myself? Because I was a stupid prick. I had no idea what I was doing on the streets but I had nowhere else to go either. I thought all hostels would be the same and from what I had heard through the grapevine they were worse. I had heard of people being stabbed in their sleep, gang-raped, burnt with cigarettes. When you are a fresh kid those things are as scary as fuck. I thought I had more chance of dodging that shit on the streets than in the hostel. There were other kids on the streets that still had smiles on their faces, so I thought I could do it too. But real smiles and sly smiles are two different things and I was going to learn all about it. I moved into a new nightmare of life. I started hating people. I became more and more paranoid of people who just looked at me.

What do you do when your head is filled with vi-

sions you don't want and you are too immature to deal
with the pressure? I will tell you: you run, and keep on
running from what you don't know. Where? You don't
know. All you know is something is missing and all the
colours are gone, nothing seems pretty any more. It all
seems poison, every one who looks at you is seen as a
potential predator.

Everyone handles their demons differently and I
handled mine with violence. A lot of people would be
thinking, *Why didn't you tell anyone?* Because as far as I
knew every fucker hated me. I spent ninety percent of
my time off my face, escaping reality. I spent the other
10 percent looking for the drugs to get me there. Things
seemed different when I was off my guts. I'd sit in the
park and sniff all day long and wait till the next hiding came. I figured I was fucked anyway it didn't matter
which way I went, I found trouble. I had my shoes taken
off me once and I was mobbed by a bunch of other street
kids sitting down drinking a cask of wine in the park.
We were all sitting next to a little lake, and I thought I
had made a new bunch of friends, until one with tight
curly hair smashed a glass bottle over my head. I woke
up the next day still at the lake, half in the reeds and half
out. I was a bruised mess, and wet, because I must have
been thrown into the lake as well. I don't know what
happened that night, all I know is I was bruised all up
my legs. I had sore ribs and an eye swollen shut. I spent
the next few days walking around like that, all fucked
up. Each time that kind of shit happened to me I think I
changed inside just that little bit more. I was scared shit-

less of walking around from place to place in case one of them seen me. I couldn't remember what they looked like and every one I saw with tight curly hair I'd hide from. I'd run into shops and hide behind clothes racks, anywhere I could. But I never met that bunch again.

Then one day about a week later I met a brother named Skoop. He wasn't scared of no one, and had a reputation around Perth as one of the best car thieves. I needed a real friend and he took me under his wing. He also introduced me to speed, whiz, whatever you want to call it, as well as a whole range of other pills. The first time I had speed with him I got sick. I snorted it and got the shits. We were at a house he shared with his girl-friend, Stacey. I ended up going to sleep on the couch and they went out. The next morning they came home and woke me up with some more speed. This time it was in a needle. I was nervous about it because of what happened to me the night before but they pretty much told me that it would make me feel a hell of a lot bet-ter. When I seen them do it and how they were rush-ing around, I agreed. I didn't like needles, but it didn't seem to hurt them, I put my arm out and rolled up my sleeve.

This was the biggest mistake I ever made in my life.

Stacey said to grab my arm up the top and squeeze. I did, and when she put the needle in I shut my eyes for a split second. When I opened them again I saw blood go into the needle. It all disappeared into my vein.

She said, "Let go." I did and boom! It hit me like a tonne of bricks. The hair on the back of my neck stood up, my heart felt like it was going to jump out of my chest, everything seemed real. I thought I had special senses but really I was paranoid. All my problems in life weren't problems anymore, they were an excuse to get off my face and hide in a false state of mind.

I started talking faster and grinding my teeth. The feeling for me—someone who was getting around feeling like a miserable waste of time—was fucking incredible. There was the difference between a sly smile and a real smile, and I was now wearing the sly smile too.

The first day I met Skoop I thought he was cool. He looked like a scary prick, but there was something about him that was easy-going. I wondered to myself, Would this fella help me if I was in trouble, like a big brother would? His cousins had told me all about him smashing people and shit. People don't fuck with him, so I guess in a way I was looking for some protection. I was sniffing glue with some Noongar kids. I was off my face on glue and feeling invincible. He'd just got out of court and told his cousin to hand him his screwdriver. I was wondering what the fuck he needed a screwdriver for.

He said, "There's an SLR 5000 over there in the car park. Youse can have it if you want. I'm getting this darty thing just outside the court."

Now I wasn't sure but I loved cars and driving and any shit with motors in it. I learnt how to drive at Dad's work, moving cars around to wash them. The fastest I ever got was 30 kilometres. But I jumped up and said, "Brother, I'm the best driver here. Let me take the car you don't want. Just, how do I start it?"

He looked at me and said, "You reckon you can drive and you can't even start it?" He took me over and I was shitting myself with excitement, butterflies in my stomach. Part of me didn't believe it and part of me just said, "Let's go!" The car was red and black with all the flare kit. I looked inside and I could see the plastic over the steering column was busted. He was in the car in three seconds.

He said, "You reckon you can handle this thing, brother?"

I gulped and said, "Fuck, yeah."

I had driven Dad's beach buggy (a manual) when we went beach-buggying and I thought, Can't be too hard...

Skoop said, "Jump in the other side."

I did without a second to lose. Then he pushed this pin down: the red lights in the dash came on; he pumped the accelerator a few times; vrooooooom! The thing sounded fucken mean. I nearly shit my pants. I hadn't even got my seat belt on properly and we were in a full drift sideways out of the car park, onto the street leading to the city.

Skoop eyeballed me and said, "I'll jump out just up here. You follow me in this when I pull out. Okay?"

"Okay."

I was shaking like a rattle. No bullshit, not three minutes after he jumped out of the car I heard this rumble, and with a screech from hell a white V8SS fully bombed machine came speeding out sideways from the car park and ended up facing me. All I saw was this great big grin.

I revved the accelerator and let the clutch out; the car jumped and I was off. I could see his brake lights waiting for me. I made a few mistakes changing gears. *Cleaning the teeth* we called it, but I figured it out quickly. I stalled a couple of times and shit myself because I didn't want to get caught. I pushed the pin down and it started again. It wasn't long before I was flying around corners, losing control, being a dickhead. In actual fact, because I didn't care what happened to me, it was like I was possessed. My foot would just push harder and harder. I was playing chasey with Skoop and loving it, not thinking of the lives I was putting at risk. Driving the car the way I was, it was an escape from reality. I had no worries, shut off from the outside world.

That was the very beginning. I ended up stealing cars day and night all different shapes and sizes had them parked all over the place. Some nights if I didn't know how to steal a certain car I'd make it my mission to learn and I learnt fast. The best thing about cars was the inside: I was guaranteed a warm night of sleep as long as I had a screwdriver. I done my apprenticeship keeping a lookout, busting into the cars, getting sprung and running off all I heard was, "Oi! You little cunt—that's my car!" Depending how far we had to go till the car was started, we'd either choose to stay and start it or bail and jump out.

We had so many close calls. One time some dude smashed his own windscreen with a baseball bat. Lucky for us the car started. We were out of there—high speed chases all over Perth. I thought I was the best because I

41

hadn't been caught yet. My first chase was with Skoop. We were in an SLE Commodore automatic. I was nervous as hell, but I hung on like flies to shit. Skoop was crazy: he drove straight through parks, over copper logs, he didn't give a fuck. He done anything to get away from the police. I'd be shitting myself but adrenaline kept me going strong. I got used to it; a whole different rush to the drugs. Skoop taught me how to not give a fuck. I seen him knock blocks clean out because he didn't back down from no one. He even took gear off the dealers in the city and I loved that shit because they were dogs to me whenever they saw me. But not when I was with Skoop. They sucked up my arse, then. My shoes were fucked one day and Skoop got me a brand new pair off one of the dealers in town, but we never paid for them and they hated me for it. As long as I was with him I didn't care. Skoop got caught one night in a high-speed chase. He crashed the car and ended up in hospital. He'd broken a leg when he hit a lamppost and the police car rammed him. Four years for that. I'd been at the other end of the city snooping around.

Skoop was also the first person I stabbed. One night when we were off our guts on speed, we went out stealing cars. I was still 14 years old. We took some cerepax we got from his old lady's house. She had all sorts of pills and was always off her guts, so she never knew we took them. This particular day we took a lot of them. Actually, I took about six, and I don't know how many Skoop had, but we were off our faces. One minute I'd be somewhere and the next I'd snap out of it again. I'd lost a couple of hours and had no idea how I got to wherever I was. I was spinning out, thinking I was going to die because I hadn't taken any pills at all up until now. I remembered seeing Mum OD-ing on pills. I think one of the reasons I took them was because I thought: *I'll show you, Mum. If I die it's your fault.* I didn't want to die, but I didn't give a fuck if I did. I wanted to see how they would react if I was dead, but if I was dead then it wouldn't matter how they reacted. My head was a fucken mess. I wanted my mother to feel my pain and suffer like I was. The truth of it all, though, was that I just wanted attention.

Me and Skoop ended up in a Perth block of flats near Herds man Parade. We were sitting in some Kingswood, trying to steal it, and I said, "Let me have a go." That's all I said, and *whack!* I got stabbed in the top of my head with a screwdriver and fuck it hurt. I had my own screwdriver and automatically pushed it into his leg. I started saying, "Sorry, bro, I didn't mean it. Why did you stab my head?" But the prick started laughing at me. Then he frightened me, saying,   "You're gone."

That was it for me—I was out of there. I'd never done nothing like that and never had nothing like that done to me. It didn't feel like nothing. My fucken head hurt, that was all I knew. As I took off, Skoop was yelling, "You 'right, bruz? Come back here!"

I said, "Nah, fuck that. See ya." I went my own way, crying and spinning out, thinking I could have been killed. He was my mate, and just like that he stabbed me in the head. Where could I go from here? Who could I trust now? No one.

I had a raging drug habit after two weeks of being on the gear-speed-whizz with Skoop. When I left that night I had no idea what life had in store for me. I'd met a couple of dealers when I was cruising around with Skoop, and I knew where they lived. There was, for example, always someone on the Joondalup train line heading out to score. They stood out like dogs balls—AS ALL JUNKIES DO. All I had to do was come up with the cash. One hundred dollars done me alright: that was a gram back then. Enough for me to get off my head about four times. I didn't have the biggest habit, and I'd had good gear, not the shit that's out there these days. That just head-fucks you. Back then, when I was fourteen, the shit made you rush around like a chook with its head cut off. When I woke up in the mornings (that's if I slept) I had to go find some way of getting on. For me, shoplifting was the best bet. When I was older I would till snatch, or sometimes friends done ram raids and I'd follow, loading the cars up. They'd drive straight through the front doors of a shop and load the car up with whatever stock was available. Then we'd drive to a dealer's house, swapping the goods for speed. Some houses were like drive-through bottle-shops. It wasn't no syndicate, just a bunch of young punks like myself getting paid and blue at the same time. We sold it to other alcoholics around the Bronx. Back then I thought I was doing my

◀ Air brush painting, tin
*I did this in 2005 whilst off my head. I'd been awake for about
2 weeks and I realised that I was angry at that stage in my life
but going through a changing phase.*

45

fellow pissheads a good turn. I thought I was making life easy for some people, but now I see all I was doing was feeding two habits: mine and theirs. Only I had to pay full price for the shit I was on.

I'd steal cars, but it didn't seem like I was doing anything wrong. I didn't feel anything for the person whose car it was because I didn't know them. It was just the same as stealing a Mars Bar from a shop, only I didn't stick the car down me pants. I found out how serious it was, though, after I was chased through the suburb of Southlakes, only getting away by the skin of my balls. It was that close, I could smell the persons BO. I was trying to steal this little bomb of a Kingswood and suddenly someone came running from the side of the house. I heard him yell, 'I'll fucken kill you, you little prick!" The bloke was in his jocks. I shat myself, opened the door, jumped out and ran. This dude, if he hadn't been so big, would have caught me, too. I ran like I had a hound chasing my arse. He kicked me in my arse, he was that close. I yelled, "Fuck off!" I could almost feel his hands reaching to grab me – so close – when he fell over something. I thanked God and ran even faster. When I saw he was down for a second I ran straight up this alleyway to a house with no fence. I ran into the backyard and hid under the wheelbarrow like a turtle. I curled myself as tight as a ball. Waited. Not even a minute later, I seen his feet next to my head. I could have snorted a line of coke off his big toe. I thought I was fucked. If he lifted the barrow I was going to get the absolute shit kicked out of me. But something was on my side that night. I watched as his feet took off back the way we came. I didn't move for at least two hours after that I fell asleep, still a turtle.

They were the nights I'd settle for a Salvo bin. Good on the Salvos. When I did get a car I'd drive to the bush just up from Mum's house in Yangebup and sleep in it. Or I'd park at the shopping centre in Yangebup and sleep in the Salvo bin, depending on how full it was. I learnt a lot of things from living in bins full of clothes: falling asleep with a candle burning is the wrong thing to do. I escaped from that bin by a matter of seconds. I'd been sitting in the bin, drawing a picture in my little book I carried with me. I had a candle I had stolen from the Farmer Jack's store, as well as a couple of blocks of chocolate (Cadbury chocolate mint). The thing that woke me up was the instant warmth and light in the bin. The clothes went up like petrol was poured on them. Smoke filled the bin and I coughed my lungs up. I booted the door and it flung open. I just got out, falling over at the door. I got up and ran, still half asleep. My book was burnt, and so was my chocolate. I went and hid in the bush up the road a little bit. I heard sirens coming and about ten minutes later a spot light came shining through the bush, really slowly. I hid underneath a blackboy plant, freaking out, thinking I was going to get eaten by ants and spiders. All the spikes sticking in my back from the plant were sending shivers up my spine, because it felt like I had things crawling on me. I was praying to God, please don't let me get caught, please, please, please. It would've been around one o'clock in the morning.

Later I walked into the next suburb and found a 24-

hour service station because I wanted to steal some more chocolate. But the dude was suss about me, and told me to leave if I wasn't buying something.

"It's past your bedtime," he said.

I just looked at the Coca-Cola clock and it was three o'clock. I told him to get fucked and walked out. I wanted to yell all sorts of shit at him, like, "If I had a fucken bed I'd be in the thing, you curry munching cunt."

Another lesson is don't sleep in the bins if it's got a buggered latch. It's embarrassing when you get stuck halfway out the latch and the door of the whole thing swings open. Half of you hanging out one side and half out the other. People walk past to go shopping and *voilà*: there you are, stuck swinging in the wind. That was pretty funny, even I pissed myself laughing when that happened. But if you got in there at the right time of the week you got some good nights sleep. When people stuffed kid's toys and things in there it was sometimes better sleeping somewhere else. I slept in slides at parks, and in the round tunnel tubes. If I had no blankets the moisture of the night used to piss me off. By the time the sun came up my clothes were damp and I'd be freezing my balls off. You know that feeling on a cold night when you first lay in your bed and you shiver like all shit until your body heat warms the bed? Well, that's what it feels like only there's no bed and no blankets. I'd pull my jumper down over my knees and pull my head back in the neck hole. My breath would warm me up a little bit. I always used to imagine my nice warm bed at home and wish there was some way I could wake up and it all be a dream. But it was no dream.

Sometimes I slept out the back of the bakery in Yange-bup, on milk crates piled up against the wall. The wall was warm and the baker, Bob, used to give me a fresh pie every now and then. I met him at the back of the shops when I was sitting there one time, early in the morning. Mum's house was only a ten-minute walk from the shops. I guess that was why I chose to hang around there when I found my life on the streets. I always retreated to my mum's suburb when things went bad in the city. Bob used to sit and listen to some of my stories. I mainly hung shit on my parents to try to get him to feel sorry for me. I think he always offered me a pie when he saw me because he knew I would be hungry. He wasn't far from right, either.

When people, usually just passers by, used to ask what I was doing out at that time of night I would change my answer depending on the person. I'd tell them to either mind their own business, or if I thought they were police I'd bullshit and say I was waiting for my mum. But they soon learnt I was on the streets. I would pop up at the wrong places at the wrong times, wearing the same clothes and with the same answer every time I was caught. They'd just take me to a hostel or the police station. I'd go in the back of the police van, with the officers thinking they were race-car drivers; going around corners flat out, throwing me around the back of the van. Whenever we got to the hostel I would just take off again as soon as the police left. If you misbehaved at the hostel you were kicked out, and I was misbehaving all the time: all the drugs I was taking and the crime I was doing. I didn't like police because as far as I was concerned they were arseholes. I'd been done for stealing a knife from school, and a couple of times for smoking and swearing at the front of shopping centres. They knew I was up to no good. Most of the time the people I was seen getting around with didn't help my cause at all. The police and me didn't get on. It was drummed into my head: they were dogs. Lock you up quick as look at you. I heard plenty of rumours about other street criminals going missing. Whether they were tales or not, I wasn't taking no chances. I'd heard all about them flogging car thieves with phone books and typewriters. Everything negative a police officer could do I had heard of them doing. To them, my kind was just a street rat. How do I know that? Because they told me. Anytime they told me to move along out of a door way or at a train station.

I slept and walked wherever I could. Toilets, community halls. When it was cold you went anywhere with shelter. Some nights I would just sit somewhere and draw either on myself with pen or on bits of pizza boxes or in my little drawing pad I always had. I drew a lot with dots back then. I used a fine tip Artline and built pictures up: mainly all evil screaming mouths, faces melting. I always wanted to try to put as much as I could in one picture. I wanted pain on paper. Even today I still haven't done a picture that I am completely happy with. I like them all but I know I can smash a boundary. I'd sit and draw, too scared to go to sleep. I'd still end up nodding off, though.

I'd sometimes think of my parents when I saw a car like theirs, or smelt certain smells in the air. I'd ring my mum and tell her I was going to kill myself and tell her it's all her fault. I was hoping they would show some feelings but all my mum could say was, "You do what you have to do," and hang up on me. When she said that I couldn't understand how she could say it. This person who gave birth to me didn't like me, miss me, or even think of me. I loved my mum. Deep down, all I wanted was to sit with her and talk. Whenever I got her on the phone I'd start off crying, saying I wanted to come home, but soon I'd hear Mum say, "It's a bit late for that now. Peter won't have it. Wayne, you blew it. Did you break into your father's workshop?" Then I'd lose the plot and start yelling at her. "If I broke into the place it would have fucken burnt to the ground. Why did you do this to me, Mum? Why did you let me go like this?"

Mum would deny any involvement, saying, "You done this to yourself, Wayne."

"You fucken bashed me, bitch, and you know you did. You made that fat cunt hit me. Call you a bitch? You are a fucken bitch! Look at what you did. You can get smart on the phone all you like but you know, Mum, and one day you will pay for all this shit. I've been tortured, fucked with and mentally destroyed. You're all gonna get yours. You lied to Dad to get him to flog me. I hate you, cunt!"

I hung the phone up and smashed it to pieces. I'd scream down the phone shit that was happening on the street but no one would believe me. They thought I was just trying to get attention. I'd walk around after that in a wild state, just wanting to break something. I remembered my bed at home and I'd hate my brother Pinkie even more, because he was at home sleeping in it.

As you can see I didn't kill myself either. I was a mess, though. I'd sit near phone boxes some nights and plan for hours exactly what I was going to say to Mum. I'd want to say sorry for talking to her like shit, but every time I did I went wild again and said all the things I was trying to avoid. I sat in the bush some nights, just up from Mum's house, and watched till the lights went off. I'd go through all sorts of thought patterns. I'd miss Mum, then I'd hate her. I'd imagine I was a sniper out of the Rambo movie, waiting for my target. I'd sit there looking at her house, talking to it, throwing questions I knew they couldn't hear.

When I had enough of sitting around feeling sorry for myself I got up and walked around, breaking into cars, looking for change in the ashtrays or mobile phones on the dash. I started thinking of my granny and my aunties in Albany. I decided I'd hitchhike down there. I didn't want to steal a car because my gut feeling was against it. It was a long drive and I hadn't driven that far before on my own, so I chose to hitch. It wasn't too hard, but it was a bit scary. I got used to it, though. People were usually pretty good with giving me lifts. Some nice people, some weird people. And by weird, I mean I thought I was sitting in the car with a robot. The dude didn't talk, and when he did it sounded like his voice was recorded. But then again I was young, I had drugs in my system and I was sleep deprived - or he could have been a robot.

Most of the people that gave me a lift couldn't believe how old I was. It was cool, because I could be whoever I wanted them to think I was. I told heaps of bullshit stories that no doubt they knew where bullshit. I'd say things like: I was going to race motor cross and my bikes and things were already in Albany at my uncle's. I think back now and feel stupid. I must have looked like a dickhead, but people acted like they believed me. Some people bought me a feed, like a sausage roll and a drink. I liked it when people done things like that for me, because I knew I could go on another day and I always felt good with food in my stomach. As a little fella does, I gave off little hints if I was hungry to try get the people to pull over and get something for me. I didn't like asking for things in Mum and Dad's house. In their house it was rude if you asked for things—you waited until it was offered.

One car picked me up and it was some fella on the way home from working away. He had some pot, mull, weed, dope, buds, whatever you want to call it. I got that stoned, I started getting paranoid on the dude driving the car. All because he was not talking. So I asked him to let me out. He spun out a little, but he was in a hurry to get home, so he took off again. I waited about an hour then started hitchhiking again. Running from my mind. When I reached Albany, I moved to my Auntie Jeanette and my Uncle Jeff's house in Spencer Park. There were also my cousins Darrel and Bradley.

I started working for my uncle, who ripped me right off. I worked on his boat, fishing in the Albany harbour. I got up at five every morning and went to work pulling in nets by hand. It was tough work, fingers getting bitten by crabs and spiked by bream six hours every day for about six weeks. All I ever got was a packet of cigarettes.

I started hearing voices out on the boat. I even thought I heard my brother's voice calling me names and whispering to me. I put it down to the salt water. I shit myself wondering what was wrong with me. I thought I was crazy, because I knew the voices weren't real. I told my uncle what happened.

He freaked out and said, "You been smoking that green shit?"

And believe it or not, I hadn't. I was just going nuts. I thought I was making it up. It didn't happen often, just when I was in dead silence. It used to scare me but I'd block it out by talking absolute shit over the top, drowning it out. It worked for me. But my uncle didn't quite know what got into me.

"Good," I said. "Keep you on your toes."

I didn't hear voices telling me to do fucked up shit, just voices calling me names. I don't know what it was that was happening to me. I'm no doctor. I was just fucked up from sniffing the glue and petrol. My uncle didn't trust me at all. None of my family did. Whenever I used to ask, "When am I getting paid?" I got made to feel uncomfortable, and Jeff would say, "When I get my cheque, then you'll get paid."

Well, he must have never got that cheque.

But it was okay, I guess. He did have a great big five-bedroom house. Two bathrooms, two cars, three fishing boats. I had nothing. But I guess he needed it more. Jeff, I still remember you.

My auntie was a dead-set bitch, always moody at me because she had a problem with looking out for her sister's kid. I'd ask if I could eat something and I always felt like it was a problem feeding me. They didn't really want me at their house. I didn't even like going to the toilet at their house because I thought it would stink too much.

My cousin Darrel, her oldest son, was just as bad as her. He was a thieving prick. He stole money off his parents, my other aunties, anyone he could. And I got the blame. Like I didn't have enough problems of my own. I nearly had punch-ons with my aunties and uncles over that. Darrel was a strong-looking boy because he'd worked on fishing boats his whole life. He'd get me to draw all designs on him with a pen and he'd get around for days with them on him. I liked doing that. He was so full of shit he used to ring girls, telling them he was getting a tattoo, but it made me feel good because everyone liked my pictures.

One night Darrel dumped me halfway between Albany and Perth. In the middle of the night we were in this panel van with about four other people, all getting pissed driving to Perth with two girls we'd met at the Albany train station. My cousin's mate was driving. Darrel was seventeen and I was still fourteen. Some argument broke out, because they were using my money. He was showing off in front of the two girls in the car and talking to me like shit. I was not happy. So I told him to get fucked. We pulled over and he punched the fuck out of me. They took off, leaving me on the side of the road in the middle of nowhere. The police came along and picked me up, then took me to a hospital in some little town. I was released the next day with a bus ticket back to Albany. Nothing ever happened to my cousin because I never gave him up.

They still owe me money. No drugs, no nothing, has hidden that. All the drugs I have put through my body didn't help me to escape that shit, all they done was chemically incarcerate me. My memories are like it was only yesterday.

I ended up moving out of their house after a couple of weeks. I thought they only wanted me for the Welfare money. I'd like to see them say they didn't. I could feel the pressure.

I moved from house to house. I stayed with another auntie but left because Darrel stole their phone money. I stayed with one of Mum's old friends from Albany, but I messed that up. Her oldest son used to save all his money from working on the boats, and I stole some of it one day. It was a fair bit, about three hundred dollars. I spent it all on lollies and other kid things. He found out that I had stolen it and kicked my arse for me. So I left that house, too. I felt like a lowlife piece of shit. I fucked over people who were trying to help me. All kinds of shit started happening to me from my bad Karma. I moved in with some Noongar family. I'd met them in Albany at Mount Lockyer. They had a house on Townsend Street: the same street that I had started life on. They saw me bumming around with some of their younger nephews and asked what I was doing living on the streets. They seemed like cool people. One of them was Regina. She was quiet, just trying to get her life together. She was always at work and when she was home she stayed in bed. She was a moody woman, too. Sometimes she was nice, and then other times she was just a bitch.

The man of the house was an ex-street kid, whose Dad had been in jail for life. They seemed nice and like they wanted to help me. They said they were in the pro-

▲ Tattoo of female Indian done in 2007 on a friend—Matt's arm, it was a cover up.

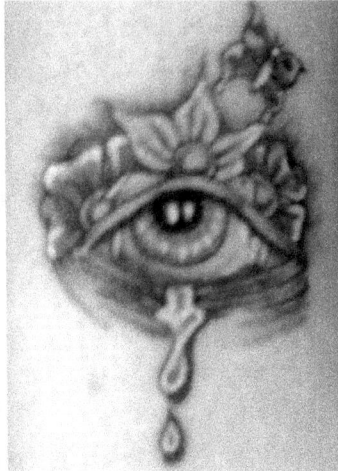

▲ Free hand tattoo of eyeball on a female's ankle (Michelle). Done in 2007 another cover up tattoo over an old name.

cess of going through a foster-parent scheme with the government. They weren't real foster parents, they just called themselves that to feel important. They saw me as a paycheque for $150 a fortnight. If I didn't spend my $60 quick they always borrowed it and I didn't get it back.

I turned into a thing for one of the guys, Quinn, to slave around the house and to try and play with sexually. One night, I had to sleep in Quinn's bed, because all the couches and other mattresses were taken by drunk relatives. I woke up one night next to this big curly-headed Noongar with his hand on my dick. I froze. Hearing him moan in my ear, I started flipping out. I jumped out of the bed and said, "What are you doing, man?" He just acted like I was spinning out. After that night I started freaking out, snapping, calling him a dirty prick. The feeling was a whole different feeling of helplessness. I wondered if I was giving off some sign that I wanted to be touched. *What was I doing to make all this shit happen to me?* I wasn't gay. I don't like men in that way at all. *What was wrong with me?* I felt dirty, ashamed, embarrassed, with a twist of hate. Quinny thought he was a gangster, because he had a bunch of dumb pricks following him around. He was about one hundred kilos to me, back then, he was a scary bloke. I weighed a maximum of fifty. But ask me now what I think: he was a dead-set weak prick. I tried to run away a couple of times, but the cousins chased me through the bush on the other side of Townsend Street. I was crying to myself: *Why is this happening to me? Everyone I trust keeps fucking me over.* I nearly got to the houses on the other side of the bush but I fell and slid along the ground. Rickie Williams was the oldest kid's name. He was also known for a rape and stabbing people. He was a freckly-faced redhead. He had been through detention centres and only just got out. He got off on the fear in my eyes, I think, because he would always say he was going to get me and flash knives at me, or he would just run his index finger across his neck while looking at me. He was my newest fear in Albany. My new nightmare: him and his whole family. He ran straight up and booted me in the face I was out like a light. All I saw was a white flash in my head and from there it was stars, just like in cartoons. He and his cousins dragged me back to the house, and dropped me down on the front porch. All of them were standing around, saying shit like, "Where you gonna go? Quinn wouldn't touch a skinny little white boy like you." I got another punch to my face. I buckled up on the porch, curling into a ball.

One of them said, "We'll chuck you off the gap, you little cunt. Don't come around here talking your shit."

The gap is a cliff at the edge of the sea. I just sat there shaking, wondering what they were going to do next, if they were really going to do it.

Quinn looked at me and said, "You can run, boy, but I'll catch you and every time I do I will make you piss, you little dog. All my cousins will flog you. Everyone will flog you." He smashed me in the face again and there were more stars. I stayed curled up. I just wanted to jump up and bite his nose off his face, but I was scared. I

59

wanted to kill the lot of them. My face was all puffed up. I had grazes up both my legs and on my lower back from being dragged. I just wanted to scream, *You dog cunts!* to all of them. I heard the scuffle of footsteps and tensed up, waiting for another kicking. But it didn't happen. They left, except for the so-called foster dad: he came out and sat next to me, saying, "All this shit is because we're trying to help you, Wayne. But you just can't see it like that." He was full of shit, but because he was being nice I listened. At least while he was telling lies I wasn't getting punched into. The next day they were all getting pissed in the backyard and I was still moping around. The next-door neighbour was over drinking as well.

He looked at me and said, "Get your chin up."

I lost it and said, "Get your own chin up, fuckhead." I pushed him in the chest and tried to throw a punch but I failed and missed. He side-stepped me and punched me in the jaw, then spun me around in a weird hold so my hands were stuck behind my back.

"Look hear, you fellas!" he said.

I was twisting and trying to get out, but each time I moved it hurt my arms. Everybody looked at me and started laughing.

One of the young cousins, Deany, came over and said, "What you being a funny cunt for?" and punched me in the guts, winding me. I felt sick and dropped to the floor. I crawled back inside and lay on the couch. About an hour later they came and shaved my head bald and eyebrows off. I tried to fight them, but I gave in and just lay there. It was better that way. At least I didn't get flogged. They had me screwed: all my money had been spent and it was another two weeks before I got paid. I was fucked in a fucked situation.

They used to make me think they were doing me a big favour, but really I was just someone for them to take all their life's frustrations out on. I lived on my tippy-toes. I didn't want to stay.

I started tattooing myself at that house with just a matchstick and two needles with cotton wrapped around them. I tattooed *Pigs Suck* on my left forearm in big letters. I'd just sit out the front on the steps with my bottle of Indian ink and tattoo. I tattooed the word *Mum* on my right knee, and a finger pulling the bird on my shoulder. That was the same time I started taking Advil car-sickness pills. One of the other boys I met on the streets in Albany introduced me to them. You could buy them over the counter at any chemist. I'd buy a bottle of fifty and take ten pills straight out of the bottle. Scared I might have taken too many but at the same time not caring, I'd start to panic as they would take effect. It would send me into a bad trip. At least when I was that off my face, everyone left me alone, thinking I was crazy, sitting talking to myself. I could actually see people there; they were figures of my mum and dad, my brother, Quinn, Donna, Chris, Skoop—all the people that played a part in my life. People were pulling guns on me, saying they were going to fuck my dead body. That's what I heard when I was off my guts. I saw people up the end of the hall with shotguns pointed at me. Little monster-looking things, about knee-high, which followed me everywhere. My pants felt like I had constantly shit myself. Anything that I thought in my head happened. Well, it seemed real. I was depressed, angry, lost and scared. All those things, mixed with a drug that was completely off its fucking nut, meant a holiday in Hell, and that's what I had. I'd stare at walls, just freaking out. Whatever I looked at turned evil. Faces came out of the walls. People with demon heads appeared. I could see people standing there, whispering to each other, saying they were going to throw me off the gap. Everything that had happened to me in life was there in front of me. Everyone I was ever scared of was there in my mind. So much for escaping my nightmares; it highlighted them. The other kids I was hanging with were taking them and it helped me get over the speed when I got to the town. I was a stupid kid, now that I look back. Some of the shit I done and the excuses I made for myself were just absolute bullshit. Immaturity is what was really going on, mixed with all the other shit.

Then one night me and a friend stole a car in Albany, and wouldn't you know it: I got caught. It was a VN Commodore Station Wagon. I had another young mate in Albany, his name was Wayne as well. He had never stolen cars or anything like that, and I was leading him into a world of shit. He went to school and told some kids where I stashed the car, and one of them was the local coppa's son. That afternoon the police came to the house I was staying at and arrested me. I was then taken to the police station and charged. The police tried scaring me with stories of what was going to happen if I didn't stop stealing cars, but I didn't believe them. I knew everything. Unfortunately for me, that was it. I ran out of luck and I was sent to Longmore Remand Detention Centre for the first time.

PLEASE

Excuse me sir do you have a spare dollar
veins popping out
Sweat on the collar
That I do want one or two
What happened next
Is left to you
I never sold myself once
I was no hooker
Dirty old dog
Was a high class booker
Hunting for kids
Children for bids
Pack of the pricks
Dirty old fiddlers
Drawin' kids into cars
I seen the shit
But never played the card
Girls coming back tears in their eyes
Blood fucken noses
Bruises on their thighs
They got ours so we got theirs
They hunted in packs we stalked in pairs
Wrong or right
There was pain that night
Scarred us enough
So we pulled the noose tight

Wayne McKay

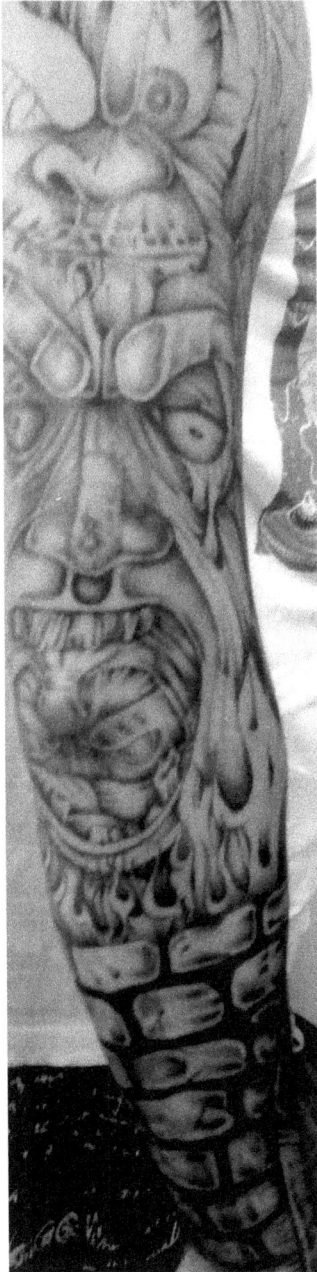

3

MY FAMILY ON THE INSIDE

The system says institutions rehabilitate. The idea is that they are supposed to teach young people how to live a normal lifestyle. I didn't see it like that at all. I saw it as a crime lab. A place to meet other criminals.

My first time in detention, I was taken from Albany to Perth. I had warrants for my arrest for stealing cars. My accomplices gave me up cold, telling the police. That was a shock to me.

I didn't think that happened at all. No one told me about that shit.

My first time in the lock-up was an experience. I thought I was a hard little prick, swearing at the police like I was an adult. I hated them and their uniforms. Well, I didn't really, I was just told that's the best thing to do. I got a good slapping from one of the coppers and I still didn't learn. I'd had the fuck punched out of me on the streets, so his bitch-slaps were like having my grandma slap me. They thought they would scare me but it didn't work. They were trying to get me to admit to taking cars I didn't even steal. I didn't even know the suburbs they were stolen from.

Then it was off to Longmore Detention Centre, and to be honest I was shitting myself. Mum and Dad had driven me past this place and said that this was where I was going to end up. It was a place for boys and girls that kept fucking up, for stealing cars, armed robbery, murder, rape, paedophilia, arson, manslaughter: you name it, they done it. It was a frightening experience, not knowing what to expect, hearing rumours that people get bashed, stabbed and raped. And people spit in the food. All in all, I will be honest: I just wanted to go home. I didn't care if they hated me, I just wanted to go home. The police rang my mum and asked if they would bail me out, and the answer was *No*. So it was off into the jungle for me. I was in there for two weeks, which seemed like forever.

We drove in through steel gates and up to a roller door. The roller door didn't open until the gates had shut behind us. My heart was beating like crazy. I was basically expecting that as soon as the doors opened and we walked in I was going to get raped and smashed, but it was not like that at all. Instead, a short, stocky Aboriginal worker with a bit of a put-on attitude came up. He was trying to act all hard, but he was actually not a bad group worker. It was just while the police were there, I think, that he tried to act all staunch. He could sense I was shitting myself, and started making jokes at me, telling me I would be safe, I was going into the girls section to share a cell with four girls. I smiled a fake smile and just kept walking up this long, grey corridor. Door lined both sides, about six feet apart, with little square glass peepholes.

There were about twenty on each side. It smelt like cleaning products and mould mixed together. It felt like I was in a bad movie.

The group worker told me that they were the cells for the girls. The wing was so quiet you could hear a pin drop. Outside every door there was a fresh roll of toilet paper. Some of the doors had a pair of thongs and some didn't. We came to the end of the wing and stopped. The worker had a big bunch of keys, he rattled around and found the key he was looking for. The door opened and we walked into the shower block. That was where the mould smell was coming from. The steam floated up the wings when they had shower times. In the wall was a little square roller door that was open. I could hear voices yelling and laughing and basketballs bouncing. The outside recreation centre was just the other side of the doors. The worker then told me to strip. I was a bit embarrassed. I heard a voice yell, "What size clothes, boss?"

The worker yelled back, "Long and skinny."

I had a complex about my weight as it was, and hearing that didn't help me at all. I just stood there naked, and waited to be told what to do next. The worker then put on some white gloves and that was it for me.

I said, "What the fuck are those for, man?"

The worker saw it coming and laughed at me.

He said, "It only hurts a little bit. You'll be right."

"No way, man. You're not doing that shit to me." I thought he was going to stick his finger up my arse. But that was not the case, thank God. I was told to squat and cough, lift up my feet, wiggle my toes, turn around and face him, lift up my tongue, run my fingers through my hair. As I was doing this, a young kid about sixteen walked around the corner with a pile of clothes and a towel, as well as two laundry bags full of clothes and toiletries. All of a sudden the showers turned on.

The worker walked over with a bottle in his hand and said, "Rub this through your hair." He squirted a bit in my hair and said, "You get five minutes in the shower, then I turn them off. I will call, 'Ten seconds to go,' and you will know when to rinse off."

I was feeling a little more relaxed after the shower. I dressed and was told to follow the worker again. We went to a room with lots of tables and chairs: the visitor's centre. I was told to sit at one of the little desks. I waited there for about five minutes, with all my new clothes in the bags. I was nervous again, waiting for the next step. A little old man walked out. He had glasses and looked like a gentle old bloke, but I was wrong. He had the shits with the world.

He told me straight out, "We don't fuck around here. You call us either boss, miss, or sir. T-shirts tucked in at all times. Footwear is to be worn at all times. No swearing. No fighting. No bullying. No smoking. All inmates have to work or do education. Unlock is at seven o'clock, and lock up is the same. Wednesday is an all-day lock-down, because we have staff meetings." He then asked me a whole bunch of medical questions, like: *Did I have asthma? Was I gay?*

I answered, "No," like he was putting me on.

Did I use needles? When was the last time I had a hit in the head? Was I on any medication? Had I ever threatened self-harm? Had I any tattoos? Did I have any identifiable scars? I answered yes to some and no to others. For half of them I didn't understand what he was talking about, but I just answered anyway.

He then asked if anyone knew where I was. I said no. I was allowed one phone call. I rang my uncle in Albany and started crying.

He just said, "You're a fucken idiot, aren't yah?"

And that was my phone call.

I was taken around the whole place and shown where the workshops were. It was like a big school, only it had bars on all the windows and there were alarm buttons everywhere. When we walked outside into the rec yard, there were kids from the age of ten to almost eighteen.

Next step for them: prison. All the boys were dressed in blue jeans and a green or blue t-shirt. The girls had maroon jumpers and t-shirts. I felt eyes burning through me. Everything stopped and people were whispering amongst themselves.

Now I was shitting myself. I just wanted to drop dead right there and then. This was not me. I was not supposed to be here. I was hoping it would all just be a bad dream, but it wasn't. It was all real. It's still real now, as I am writing this.

After I was shown around the place it was time for everyone to go and have tea. First we had to return to our cells. The worker told me to stay with him and he would find out what cell I was in. Those words nearly made me pass out. *A cell! What the fuck?* That was the shock of a lifetime. I walked with him behind a group of kids. Some of them were looking behind with sly expressions; they could sense I was shitting myself. We all walked through these two big doors that lead into a new corridor with cells down both sides. There were more in this wing than in the first corridor I saw. We walked halfway up and stopped. The voices were all echoing up the wing. People making car noises, baby laughs, or just screaming whatever came to mind. It was like a nuthouse. I heard the doors rattling down the wing as the workers unlocked doors so the boys could get into their cells. Then the worker with me said, "Home sweet home, boy. This is your cell." I walked into this tiny little room about six foot by eight foot, and ten foot high. There was a dirty, smelly stainless steel toilet with no lid. The bowl was stained from shit over the years and a half used toilet roll was on the floor in the corner. Against the side of the cell was a steel frame mounted to the wall with a ratty old mattress on it, and a pillow that was brown with sweat and whatever else. Names were scratched into the walls and the door. There was a little bench in the corner with about six pieces of writing paper and a lead pencil on it. Spit and who-knows-what all over the walls and roof, urine all up the wall near the toilet. There was a little stainless-steel hand-basin with bits of toilet paper in the drain. Right next to and above the toilet was something that was supposed to resemble a mirror: a little square sheet of Perspex that had scratches all through it. When I looked my face was distorted and it did not look like me at all. This was all mine.

The worker said, "There is a library here. You can go and get some books if you put your name down when they call you over the loudspeaker." There was a sheet of paper on the bench that said in big bold letters: RULES OF LONGMORE TRAINING CENTRE.

"You'll have to read that after. Get changed for dinner. The collared shirt is for dinner times. I'll be back in two minutes." He locked the door and walked down the corridor. I could hear his footsteps tapping away as he walked along the polished floor. I looked around at my surroundings again and thought to myself, *I'm not in Kansas no more.* This was definitely not a dream. I quickly lay the mattress down and pulled the sheets out of one of the bags, half unfolded it and laid it on the bed so I could tip my clothes on it. The clothes were all old. Some of the t-shirts had holes in them and paint all over them. The jocks were all too small, the socks were odd and my dinner shirt was too small, but I had to wear it. I just folded the sleeves up. The worker came back to the cell about four minutes later and said, "Come with me." He unlocked the door and I walked out.

He said, "Tuck that shirt in." So I did, fumbling like I was going to get shot if I didn't. I had no idea how to act. This was the beginning of a whole new lifestyle.

We walked to mess hall. As we approached, I could see a line coming out the door. People were playing around in the line, waiting for their turn to enter the room. Sounds of plastic chairs sliding across the floor and plates crashing echoed out of the room.

Workers yelling, "Sit down!"

Someone else yelling, "Go fuck yourself!" The whole room breaking into laughter. As the line got smaller I could see in the room. There were silver pots on all the tables with salt and pepper shakers. It looked like a little restaurant. People were staring at me and talking amongst themselves. At every table there was a worker sitting with the kids to keep it all under control. I walked up and grabbed my plate, watching what the person in front of me did. I just copied. The food was fish and chips that looked like shit. I didn't eat fish but I took my fish anyway to make it look like I wasn't being fussy. We were allowed two pieces of bread. The worker I walked in with had told me to sit at his table. There were two other kids sitting there; one was a big fat boy and the other was an Aboriginal kid that looked like he was pissed off with the world. I just looked straight at my food and started eating. The chips tasted like cardboard. Everything seemed to be okay and then out of the blue, over in the corner of the room, one of the tables went flying into the air. Food and hot tea went everywhere. The workers all jumped into action. This big tall Aboriginal kid called Big T had flipped his table for something to do. He was laughing his head off, yelling, "Come on you dogs! Come on cunts!" The workers all ran at him, tackling him to the floor. The doors to the mess hall flew open and three big workers ran in the room with belts around their waists. Hanging off the belts were all sorts of gadgets: handcuffs, batons, torches, a little square thing with a red button on it. Lots of other little pockets on the belt were shut. The men had white gloves on. Ready for business. They looked like a bunch of try-hard wannabes that couldn't get into the police force, so they went and pushed kids around instead. They ran straight over to Big T and grabbed him off the floor and carried him out. He was singing as they carried him: *I'm a nigger with an attitude.* One of the workers said, "Well, we'll see if we can sort that attitude out for you." Everybody else just turned around and started eating again. Someone came out from the kitchen and started cleaning the mess up.

When it all first happened I thought: *Fucken great: first day here and I'm going to get killed in the kitchen. There's going to be a riot.* It didn't quite go that far, though. I asked the other boys at the table what that had been about and they said he was probably just bored. I thought: *Fuck, if that's what happens here when people are bored, I'd hate to*

73

see what they do when they are pissed off.

One of the kids asked what my name was. I told him and asked theirs: one was William, Friday, and the fat boy was Moses. He was in for manslaughter: he stole a car and killed someone when he crashed it. That spun me out a bit. Friday was in for raping a nine year-old girl, but I didn't find that out until we were in Riverbank Detention Centre a couple of years later.

The big guy that flipped the table was taken to the punishment cells and did not return to the dining room that night after we had finished dinner. One of the officers walked up to the corner of the room and told everybody to be quiet. There were two big bins in the corner and the bench had been cleared of food. Two kids from the kitchen, dressed in white clothes, waited at the bench. The officer started telling one table at a time to bring their dishes up and empty all the scraps in the bin. My table was second. I just followed the lead of the others. We were then returned to our cells. It was about 5.30 in the afternoon.

While I was in there I quickly made my bed. There were two blankets; grey, woolly shit blankets with holes all through them. But they were what I had to make do with. Better than some nights on the streets.

There was a noise that frightened the shit out of me. The intercom started blaring: *Emergency button testing. Say your name and push the button on your wall.*

I said, "Are you talking to me, boss?"

A voice replied, "Yes, there's no one else there, is there?"

I said no, feeling like a dickhead. So I said my name and pushed the button. I could hear the same voice going from cell to cell. Some kids made jokes at it and others just said their last name. Then I heard keys rattling and footsteps.

A voice said, "Up against the end wall."

I looked out the window and just out the corner I could see four workers standing at a cell door about four cells down from me. One had a plate of food in his hand and the others just stood there watching. One of the men was wearing a suit.

He said to the person in the cell, "How are you feeling now?"

There was no answer. "Do you want this food or not?"

They put the food in the cell and walked back out and locked the door. Then all of a sudden I heard this *smash*.

"Stick the food up your arse dogs. Fucken dogs. All the screws take it up the arse, doo-dah, doo-dah. All the screws like it hard and fast, doo-dah doo-dah day."

The workers all stopped and turned back to the cell. The cell door started banging as loud as fuck. Whoever it was, they were kicking the door, screaming, "I'm gonna fuck your arse, your mum's arse, your wife's arse, and make your dog fuck your cat."

The workers just stood at the door smiling.

The one that handled the food said, "My wife's your mama, boy," and that was it. The cell was bouncing, then the workers all pissed themselves laughing and walked off, saying, "See ya tomorrow."

"You gonna see me dogs, you sure are."

I was safe and in my cell, but man I didn't feel safe at all. I just wanted to go home. The speaker on the wall sprung into action again.

"McKay! What activity do you want to do: TV room, pool room, basketball, or do you want to stay in your cell?"

I said, "TV room, boss."

After I said it I was kind of wishing I had just decided to stay in my cell. I heard a couple of other voices down the wing say, "TV boss," and "Basketball". I was freaking out, wondering if anyone here would know me from the streets, if any were Donna's friends. If she was here. If so, I was fucked. She would kill me in this place. I was her pet hate.

The worker came and unlocked the doors for the boys that were going to the TV room. I stepped out and stood by my door, looking up and down the wing. There were about seven of us so far. I just looked down at the ground again and waited for instructions.

Someone said, "Wayne."

I gulped, and looked up to a smile at the end of the corridor. I was spinning out now, man. *Who was this dude? How the fuck did he know my name?*

The worker yelled, "Follow!" and we followed, walking up towards the mystery kid. As I got closer I felt relief come over me: it was a friendly face. Daniel, my friend from Southlakes High School. He looked heaps different now and he had put on heaps of weight. I could see his cell was decked out as we walked past. He had a TV, towel, hangers and posters of cars all over the walls. He had been in for a while by the looks of it. It was good to see a face I knew, and he knew heaps of other people there.

Daniel said to me, "What you been up to, bro? I haven't seen you for ages."

"I been everywhere. I'm in for stealing cars and damage charges, and failing to stop for the police."

He laughed and said, "Same as me, brother I been slapping cars for ages. Now I've got eighteen months to do for it."

"I still have to go to court. This is the first time I been charged."

"You should be right. You'll get a work order to a bail hostel or family."

A big feeling of hope came over me, like I had a chance to escape. I ended up doing two weeks there, which went by okay. I went straight to the art class because it was the only thing I had a real passion to do. Being able to draw always made things a bit easier for me in gaol, and in the boy's homes somebody always wanted a card drawn or a picture of their girlfriend or family. When I was in Longmore, my art was at the stage where I could look at a picture and draw it to a close copy. I had a long way to go, but everybody always told me I was gifted. And that drove me to practice. I ended up earning a TV in my second week for good behaviour in the art class. The art teacher was not a bad fellow. He tried to push me into the art as much as he could in a week and a half. When I left there, I had about ten paintings. They were all dark and painful pictures like graveyards and skulls, evil clowns and shit like that. I liked evil art and crazy shit. I liked shocking people with really sick shit. People looked at me like a nutter because of my pictures. But that was their problem, not mine.

The one thing I liked about getting locked up was that I came in unhealthy and always left the place feeling like a king. The rush I'd get walking the gates was the best feeling. I'd put on a bit of weight and mostly I hadn't had cigarettes during the time I was locked up, it was a good feeling to be healthy.

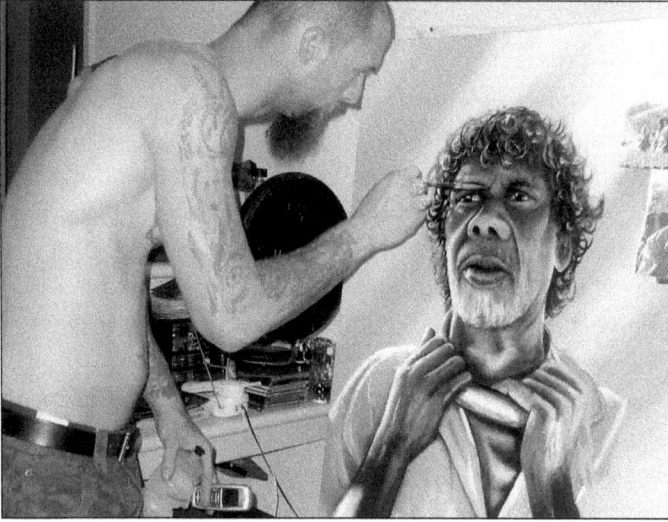

▲ *Me painting a picture of David Gulpilil. I sold the painting to his son Jida and bought a lounge suite with the money.*

◄ *The finished painting.*

ASHAMED

I twist my mind the way I know best
Igivefairwarningcoslaintliketherest
Uglylittlebirdgotkickedoutthenest
Truth in songs they call me the pest
Call me sick for the way that I think
But what thoughts are mine
And where is your link
Mymindwasmouldedthesameasyours
I was taught hate
Now I use it with a cause
Slipping away day after day
Thoughts in my head
don't seem the same way
Race against time
Running from the past
Livedoingcrimehowlongyouthinkit
will last

Lookaroundandbeashamedofyourself
We all play a part
You wanna live top shelf
Turn a cheek let the battlers seek
Gokickamanwhenyouknowhesweak
Call a cripple freak
HitthelowlevelpeakButtruthbeknown
youre the rotten leak

Live through your magazines
Go dancing with drag queens
Putitontvtellthekidswhatfagmeans
Quit smoking
Now you know they arent joking
alcohols ok
Man what you been taking

Some shit people dont need to see
Pricks watching kiddy porn
Send em all to me
givemealicencetokilllpromiselwill
do the job properly ill show you sick
thrill
I breathe in my heart beat skips
Memories of constriction
Screaming through my lips
Iknowwhatyoudonetheflashestellme
You all had fun
Less than four but more than one
If I find you dog you wanna run
I dont need no weapons

Cos bruz I am the gun

Wayne McKay

4

SEARCHING FOR A FAMILY

I was placed in a hostel in Perth called the Bail Hostel. There, they had gathered together the kids that were running amuck in the city and tried to give them different directions in life. But it was the same as all the others: fucked. So I went back to the streets. I went straight back to sniffing, popping pills and whatever else I could. I was a walking mess. I was a skinny little kid with big ears, buck teeth and long chicken legs. I looked older than I was, because I was about five foot seven.

I was harmless.

I tried to talk hard and act all tough, but I hadn't really had any fights worth calling fights. Not for much longer. I was about to meet my demon again: the butch bitch from Hell, Donna.

A guy called Scab sold me a stick of pot for twenty dollars, only he never got the twenty dollars. I didn't pay my credit, and whenever he saw me around I ran to avoid him. But one night Scab and Donna both found me walking along, acting like a big shot with one of my friends, Shorty. We had just got off the Claremont train, and it was the last train, so it must have been about eleven-thirty. We were going to see someone who Shorty knew would give us a feed. While we were walking a car pulled up and three people jumped out. We both shit ourselves. I was thinking, *What the fuck did I do?* Then I saw Scab's face. I knew what I done but I thought, *This is all about twenty bucks?*

Then I heard that butch bitch's voice. I looked around, freaking, hoping I was wrong. All of a sudden it was clear to me: I was fucked. Me and Shorty were both chucked in the boot of this stinking, smelly, stolen shit bucket. I could hear them laughing and joking around. I could feel Shorty trembling up against me. I was much the same as he was. I didn't know what to think. So many things were going through my mind. I honestly thought I was dead, and so did Shorty. The driver couldn't drive for shit: they stalled about three times (at lights, I'd say, because I could hear other cars running nearby). Every time we stopped the brake lights lit the boot up a little, and we would scream. The more we banged on the boot and yelled, the more the people in the car yelled and screamed in the front, making it sound like it was them, like they were having a great time. The exhaust fumes were nearly choking me, coming up through the rusty holes in the bottom of the floor. I felt the car turn and go over some little bumps and then all of a sudden the car stopped. A couple of seconds later the boot opened, and it was light again. It was still night but there was more light outside than there was in that tiny boot with the lid shut.

They were all staring at us. I was the one they wanted to terrorise. My little offsider was just unlucky. Three of them grabbed me out and hung me over this bridge that the train lines ran under. I was crying and wriggling, trying to get a hold of some part of the railing.

I screamed, "Help me! Someone!" and they pulled me back and started mimicking me like the kids did at school. One of the others had Shorty pinned up against the railing, saying, "Shut up, or you'll be next." Donna kicked me in the balls. I dropped to my knees. She was a cold-hearted bitch. She didn't give a fuck what she done. She grabbed me by the face. I could see all the scars up her wrists and the big bodgy tattoos.

She looked me in the eyes and said, "Bet you didn't think we'd be together again, huh? Think you can run from me, huh, you little dog?"

I didn't answer. I could see the anger in her eyes: she really fucken hated me, all after saying I was going to tell on her to the group workers.

Scab still hadn't said shit, except, "I'll teach you, you rip-off prick." He was off his face on something. He couldn't talk properly it was like he had his jaw locked shut. I told him I was sorry, and I was sorry: sorry I got caught. They kicked me around for a bit and then said,

"What are we going to do with them? We can't leave them here: they've seen our faces."

I started panicking again. Shorty was still crying to himself. I didn't blame him. I was feeling just the same as he was, only I think I had more hate in me. Hate for the butch bitch, because of what she had done to me before. I was on the edge of losing my mind. I wanted to kill her and all her weak dog friends, but if I made one wrong move I would have made shit a whole lot worse. I didn't want her to see me cry. That's why I think I was doing all right—like they say, what don't kill you makes you stronger. I was scared and in pain, there is no doubt about that, but the kicks and punches just rolled off. The words didn't bother me. I could taste blood in my mouth. I saw flashes of my little brother and sister, places I had been, precise moments in time, all flashing through my head.

Shorty was just sobbing to himself, saying, "Please, leave us alone…"

Scab pulled out a knife and held it to my throat. I gulped. I thought it was all over. He slashed it quickly across and I pissed my pants. It felt like my throat was cut, like I was bleeding and dying, but he used the blunt side of the blade.

Donna said, "You won't do the dirty ever again, will you?" and they ran off into the bushes laughing.

Shorty and I looked at each other, crying mixed with laughing. To be honest, I was still waiting for some monster to come out from the bush. I wanted out of there, but for a moment we stayed put. We heard the car take off and a bottle smash. Then they were gone.

That was the most frightening time of my life. I learnt two valuable lessons that night: don't be sly and try to dodge paying a bill and don't ever give someone up. So she was right, I wouldn't be doing the dirty again.

Shorty stopped hanging around me after that. I was almost fifteen and had already had the life frightened out of me. This shit all just made me stronger. I got around nervous and looking over my shoulder, hating the world just that bit more, and I daydreamed about revenge. I had nightmares about that night for years after, until I was nineteen or so. No doubt, so did my sidekick.

That was enough for me to take off from Perth again, so I hitchhiked back to Albany and moved into the Young House Hostel, still sniffing glue and smoking pot and popping pills. There were two older boys that were sniffing glue and petrol, but they seemed like pretty cool blokes. They were heavy metal-heads, always head-banging around the hostel. They were both named Brian. There was a pool room out the back of the hostel, where we all used to go out and sniff so the workers wouldn't catch us. Then we'd go inside, stinking of the shit, half in a coma. I'd walk around hallucinating and buzzing out of my head.

The workers always told me, "You'll end up dying of an overdose. You'll die like an addict."

I knew that, though. I was already an addict and I was contemplating death. I ended up in hospital a few times, because I'd sit up tripping out on the nightshift workers.

The food there was shit because we had to take it in turns at cooking and none of us could cook for shit. Some nights the workers would help. They were probably the nicest, out of all the hostels I went to. They sat down and talked with me when I wanted to talk to someone. But I didn't take advantage of that situation. I really should have spoken to someone back then, because my life may have turned out a little differently. If only I wasn't so filled with anger and hate. I was still receiving Young Homeless Allowance of $211 a fortnight. I'd pay my board, sixty a week, and the rest was mine. I was too generous with my money, always lending it to the other kids. Some of them used to steal my clothes. I couldn't keep hold of shit. My food would go missing from the cupboards. I'd have to hide it in my room and it started going missing from there, too. I only had noodles and lollies and things, but that wasn't the point. It was mine. I'd blow my money on shit usually, because I wasn't used to having so much money for myself, and back then $211 dollars was a whole lot of money.

I was still very immature when I was living in that hostel. I tried to throw a birthday party for myself, even though it wasn't my birthday. I hung streamers all over my room and I brought munchies and lollies. I don't know why I did it, but I did. Everyone thought I was strange anyway. I was just a kid looking for attention. I think I was trying to turn fifteen quicker. I convinced myself it was my birthday. I think about it now and I still spin out. I was pretty fucked up, man. Even I would get a bit emotional if I saw a kid doing that today. I'd be a little curious as to what was going on in their head.

Someone stole my cake. It didn't look like much of a birthday cake, but it was mine. That pissed me off to the point that I ran away from the hostel. Not that you had to run away, you could walk out. It was just a chocolate mud cake. They were my favourite cakes, and still are today, but my teeth are buggered from living off junk food and drugs, so I don't enjoy much sweet food anymore.

I never stayed away for long. When I ran away from the hostel I'd just go sit up at the *Dog Rock Café*. They were always nice to me there, and some days gave me food. I can't remember any names, but that was my hiding place. Either that, or I'd climb up on the *Dog Rock* itself and sit there until I was cold or hungry. Then I'd go back to the hostel.

Sometimes the older fellas, including the Brians, acted like they were all cool and they would take me out drinking, though they would end up punching into me. One night the two Brians and I were walking down to the main street in Albany, York Street, with a new girl from the hostel. We were all pissed on *Stones Ginger Wine*. I could barely walk, and neither could anyone else. We'd gone the back way to town so we could drink on the way. Halfway there the oldest boy told me I couldn't go no further with them. Just like that, out of the blue. I had to wait there or go home; I just couldn't go with them. I was allowed to other times. But I had no money because we had drunk it all.

I got wild with them, all except the girl, because I didn't know her properly and she didn't seem to care that I was there. I called the oldest Brian a using cunt, and that was it. They punched the living shit out of me. I was pissed and I have to say I didn't feel shit at the time. I started throwing haymaker punches at them both, but it was useless. I ate dirt again. All a part of growing up, hey? I was their boxing bag.

Sometimes they would just leave me at strange people's houses. I'd sit there in unknown company like a statue and wait for them to return, but I'd end up having to leave. I still get a bit angry about that today, because I hated the silence when I sat in other people's homes. To top it all off, one of the people was Rev, a scary looking dude with long, thick oily hair, teeth missing and tattoos. Hey, he looked a lot like me today, only I have shorter hair. I'd try to talk to Rev but he was numb. He just sat on the couch staring at the TV.

All I wanted was to be one of them, and they took advantage of it. They would use me to do all the risky shit that could end up getting me hurt or even killed. Like sending me through backyards full of dogs to look for mull plants when I didn't even know what one looked like. Doing the dirty work for them, I got bitten twice, cut my hand about five times, cuts on my face from running past things and scratching myself, twisted my ankle, and they never helped me out once. They left me wherever I fell. They were what I now call dogs.

I got alcohol poisoning and nearly died, lying on the side of the road, because those pricks were giving me Metho and wine. They wanted to see if you could get drunk on Metho. They didn't tell me what they were giving me; the doctor told me when I woke up in hospital. He said I was found on my own, dehydrated. Some lady that I never got to meet helped me. Thankyou to whoever you are: this is who I am today. I have to say, what you did for me has helped me to do a lot of gentle-natured things throughout my life. I've helped people in shopping malls that have collapsed, helped an old lady that fell out of a bus and hurt her ankle. If I see anyone lying on the side of the road that looks like they need help, I will help without a second thought. Even when I was running amuck, I still felt for people. I'd be full of shit if I said I didn't. I could switch emotion on and off when I was doing crime. If I wasn't the cause of their pain, or if it wasn't deliberate, then I felt sorry for people. I'd pull up in a stolen car and give someone a hand to jump-start their own. The people I helped, whether they thought I was too young to be driving a car or not, always said thankyou. The lady that took me to hospital saved my life, but at the time I didn't see it like that. To be honest it didn't seem like much at all. I don't think I took death seriously enough. I played with it everyday with whatever drugs I was doing at the time.

• • •

After I left the hostel I met another family in Albany through other young fellas I was hanging around with. I was still fourteen.

This house consisted of three adults. There was Uncle Donald and Auntie Daphne—I called them that because everyone else did, and I suppose it made me feel like a part of the family. But I don't remember the third one's name.

Teenagers blew in and out of the house all the time: there were about thirteen, none of them older than nineteen. My friend's names were Paul and Dion. The rest of them were their cousins. They were all really cool with me. At times I thought I was one of them: I talked their slang, ate damper on the lounge room floor wrapped in a tea-towel, with kangaroo stew and gravy in a pot. There was never food in the cupboards. We went from uncles' to aunties' houses all over Albany, getting whatever food we could scrounge up. If you went to the toilet most of the time you used phone book pages for toilet paper. All the houses were pretty much the same. All of them had holes in the walls, not very much furniture, and the beds were mattresses on the floor. Blankets were few and far between. The rooms stank of spilt beer and toe-jam and bad underarms. We would wear each other's clothes. I hated it, but that was life. These people, as nasty as they got, were still family to me, even if I was the boxing bag.

I went kangaroo hunting with them once. We went out the back of the old brickworks in Albany. About eight of us went this particular night and took a bit of alcohol with us. There were a couple of older uncles and then us boys. Peter, the eldest of the boys, was nineteen. He was tall and could run like a bullet.

The night went on and we didn't catch any kangaroos. Everyone was getting drunk. I stood up and went to piss just around the bush and this bloke in his fifties, he was just an old alcoholic, came and stood near me. I thought he was just going to do a piss. I was paranoid whenever anyone came next to me. Out of the corner of my eye I saw him flick his hand down towards my dick. I shit myself and jumped back. I felt this sting on my dick.

I panicked and yelled "Fuck! What are you doing, man? Help!" Everyone was laughing at me. I looked at my hand and there was blood all over it. The old guy had a piece of glass in his hand. I was losing it. "You fucken old dog, what did you do that for?" Then I heard a rustle from the side and everything went white – then dark. I was seeing stars.

They all kicked the fuck out of me. One of them, my so-called friend, stopped it in the end, and again I was made to feel like I had brought it on myself. In a way, I did. I suppose I chose my friends. I don't know why he had done it, the old prick, he just laughed about it like I was a weirdo making a big deal out of it. All I know is, at the exact moment he sliced I thought I'd lost my snorkel. I probably would have passed out after I yelled; no one needed to hit me. I can still see the little rock that was in front of my face when I woke up spitting dirt.

I don't know why I chose to hang around those sort of people. Sometimes the people were nice, it was just when they drank alcohol that they weren't—which was most of the time. I guess they took it out on me, or it could have been they were nice til pay day, then for a week out of the fortnight I was a piece of shit. Everyone could have a crack anytime they felt the need to hurt someone. I wished I was some Kung Fu expert so I could kick the fuck out of them all, but I wasn't so I had to make do with the old king hit every now and then. Another time the family was brawling with their in-laws, stabbing each other with knives and screwdrivers, bottles getting smashed everywhere. The police were called and they too got bashed. It ended up being a riot lasting hours. Women were pissed, crying, with cuts down their faces. Donald, one of the big uncles was punching the piss out of some Noongar police officer. Then about five officers kicked the shit out of *him*. Some prick lit his woman on fire. It was a wild house.

Once they locked me in the boot of an old Torana in the backyard for at least an hour, while they all sat around and got pissed, smashing bricks and things on the car. In that house I had to fight with one of the cousins or I got mobbed by them all. Sometimes they would be out the back punching me for what seemed like hours. I was not allowed to win. If it looked like I was going to throw a good punch I would get king hit from the side. I'd get mad at them, but that just made them all laugh at me.

I hurt this one cousin, Timmy. I didn't see him much, just when he was down from his nan's house on the other side of town. He hated my guts because I was white. He was the same age and height as me. When he came over I was already pissed out of my eyeballs. It started out okay, everyone dancing and having a good time, then all of a sudden I looked at him to see where he was, because I didn't trust him at all.

"What the fuck are you looking at?" he asked.

"Nothing."

"Are you trying to be a funny cunt, are yah? Hey?" He ripped his shirt off and charged me in the middle of the room. I wasn't copping this shit, not this night. I'd had enough and the money everyone was getting pissed on was mine. I was scared of Timmy. As soon as he was close enough I started throwing uppercuts, hoping for the best. He always had his head down when he came in and this one night I cleaned him up. I went overboard and punched the fuck out of him and it was worth every bit of the flogging I got later. To see the looks on everybody's faces when the white boy fought like a black boy and kicked ass! One of the uppercuts smashed him fair in the nose, lifting his head back, and he was out like a light. I didn't know that at the time, and I wasn't taking any chances. I don't actually re-member the flow of punches because I was too angry. All I know is, I threw a shitload that connected with his head and I was gracefully stopped with a boot to the face.

I don't remember anymore after that, except waking

up with a smashed mouth, busted ribs and lumps all over my head. And I know he didn't do them, because he was still out of it when I woke up. I was outside freezing my nuts off in the rain. I walked back inside and everyone was crying because of some shit I hadn't heard about. I just walked to the back room, had a cone and went to sleep.

Two things that family taught me: how to take a punch and give one back, and how not to treat women. The blokes in that family punched their women out all the time.

● ● ●

I had this girlfriend that I met through the family. She was a cute girl, one year older than me. Her best friend was going out with my mate, Dion, which is how I was introduced. She had gone out with Dion before, but now she was single and things looked good for me. She had dark brown hair and blue eyes and her name was Katie. I was a bit taller than she was. I hadn't known her long, but I trusted her. She was a friend.

I went to court one day for breaching a court order. When I walked in the lounge room there were about six of them standing around her with their pants at their ankles, laughing and joking. She was moaning, and pissed out of her head. They were all taking it in turns at her, like she was just a piece of meat.

That was the breaking point for me. She was the only person who I could call a friend. I was devastated.

I ran out of the house and went across the road to this lady's house where I smoked dope sometimes and I fell on the floor crying. Lying across the floor in front of me was an extension cord. I was screaming with anger. I wanted to jump out of my body and tear limbs off those pricks. The lady and man at the house had me pinned on the floor in the lounge room. They didn't know what was going on; they thought I was just losing it on drugs, saying, "What have you taken?" I looked at the cord on the floor and flicked it up with my tongue and bit it. They rang an ambulance.

I woke in hospital. You see, at the time I thought the girl was my girlfriend, but when I saw that it broke my heart. I was still a virgin. I didn't know shit about girls and the things that happened in my street were nothing compared to what I saw that day. The people in that house all knew the girl. She went to school with a couple of the boys that were there. I, to this day, think they raped her, but nothing was ever said. And I didn't say anything because I didn't know what happened.

The next day I got out of hospital. I went to the hardware store just up from the Albany hospital and stole a tube of quick grip glue. I was sick of having my head kicked in. I hated my life. After I had stolen the glue I grabbed a plastic bag off the rack and walked out of the shop. It was a ten-minute walk back to the hospital. I walked all the way, crying and mumbling to myself, swearing at God, "Why the fuck was I born? Why do you hate me?" I swore at the sky, "Kill me, take me now. I fucken hate this place." People drove past in their cars just staring at me. When I had got clear of the shops and onto a little bush track I grabbed the glue tube and started sniffing. Within about three minutes I was off my face, laughing to myself about nothing. Then I broke into a rage, talking like I was talking to people who had hurt my soul. I talked to the trees like they were people, swearing at them, telling them I would smash the fuck out of them. I took all the skin off my knuckles punching trees, then started deliberately skinning my knuckles to see the blood. I did it harder and harder, swearing at myself: *You weak cunt! Poofter! Caused it all yourself!* I still hated myself for all the shit that happened on my parents' street. It was the biggest demon I was running from. By the time I had got back near the hospital I was a walking zombie. I found a little bushy spot on the side of the road and sat there sniffing. There was a broken beer bottle that someone had thrown out the window of a car at my feet. I started thinking to myself: *I'll slash my wrists. That will show the cunts. I'll show them all. I ain't scared to die. Mum will be sorry then.* I grabbed a piece of the glass and checked to see which side was sharpest. I looked at my wrists and started slashing away at them faster and faster. I went from the bottom of my arm to the top with little slashes across my wrists. Changing hands, I did the other side. Blood went everywhere, it actually scared me. After I had done both arms and looked at what I had done, I started screaming, "I told you cunts! Now you will all be sorry." I was telling myself: *It's okay. When you die they will be fucked.* Then all of a sudden a police van pulled up and two officers came over to me.

I said, "Fuck off and leave me alone. I haven't done nothing wrong." I had glue all over me and blood was oozing out of my arms I was still crying and swearing at them.

"We want to help you."

I laughed. "Smash me, see if I give a fuck."

They asked me why I had done that to myself. All I could say was, "I've had enough of this shit."

I shouldn't have done it. I didn't achieve anything out of it, except scars on my arms and a *Self Harm* sticker on my file in the system.

• • •

I got goods and bads out of the situation. I got a warm bed for a couple of weeks. I got my health back while I was in the mental hospital. But if I had taken the time to sit and talk with someone at the hospital about what was going on in my life, instead of keeping it bottled up, I may have got the help I needed instead of just looking like an out of control child with a death-wish. I could have taken different steps. There could have been different steps from the state too. How many more signs do you need that someone is on the edge? If anyone had taken the time to put a bit of research into me they would have seen I was not just some crazy split personality kid. I had been passed off down the shit line to make it look good for the people involved. With me out of sight I was out the way. All I can say to anyone out there who feels like I felt: *Don't take it out on yourself.* Seek the help you need because you do need help and there are going to be times in your life when you look back on those moments and think, *Thank God I am still alive.*

I played the big *you coppers won't leave me alone act* and blamed everything on them. They took me straight to the hospital and I was stitched up. As hard as it may have been for me to do back then, I'll say it now: *Thankyou to the officers from the Albany police station, Western Australia, 1991, for doing that for me.*

There was an Italian lady who worked in the hospital, a nurse in her twenties. She was always really nice to me and treated me like someone who had a heart. She would bring me seconds for meals. If I didn't like the meal because it was fish or something, she would change it for me. I'd like to say thank you to her, if she remembers who I am, and let her know that I made it through life to be a father.

The next morning they released me and I did the same thing again. I slashed all the stitches they had put in me. The police came and got me again, took me back to the hospital and I was stitched up again I could sense that I was becoming a nuisance to the doctor. I didn't like him either, but I only saw him when he did his rounds. I was there because I felt safe.

Then he said, "We are sending you to a mental hospital in Perth."

I said, "No, I just want to stay here."

The lady nurse who was nice to me tried to calm me down, but I lost it, panicking.

"A mental hospital? I don't need no nuthouse."

I looked at the doctor and told him he could get fucked. "You can't make me go nowhere."

At that moment the orderlies held me down and the doctor gave me an injection.

I was sent on a plane to Graylands Mental Hospital. I woke up once on the plane halfway there, and there were three people dressed in white sitting around me. I panicked and went to move. They held me down and gave me another injection and I was out again until we were reversing into the driveway in an ambulance. The ward I was put into was a little like the Longmore Detention Centre, only there were adults getting around everywhere, seemingly off their faces. I couldn't breathe or swallow properly because my tongue was swollen and dry, side effects from the drugs that the kind doctor had given me.

From there on in the hospital they gave me needles in the arse. The rooms were different: nice, clean showers in the rooms, and clean bedding. The food was shit though, or that could have been the drugs they had me on. I don't remember too much about Graylands Mental Hospital, just that I was there for two weeks and there were some real crazy people in there with me. One lady used to strip off and run up and down the corridor. It made me laugh, watching the nurses chase her around. And she was quick! Another woman there used to talk on the phone for hours, screaming about someone killing her kids. I felt sorry for her, until I found out she had no kids. And there was no one on the other end of the phone. She was a scary women and I didn't trust her at all. Sometimes the look in her eye was evil, sometimes it was blank. So I avoided her.

I was sitting in the dining area, watching all the other people around me. I had a piece of paper and a pen and I was doodling. I don't remember what I was drawing. I got a shock when I heard them call my name. I thought it was medication time again. But it wasn't: it was a visit. Mum had come to visit! I lost the plot. I couldn't talk properly; my tongue was still swollen. I wasn't ready to see her yet. I blamed my mum for everything, for me being in this place and that I had been left to fight for myself. I was shattered that she visited, but at the same time seeing her face was nice for me. I loved her so much deep down but I didn't trust her. I was a paranoid mess. Mum could have come with all the love in the world and it wouldn't have meant shit to me. At that point there was a lot of work to be done and really neither of us wanted much to do with each other. I was too far-gone at that point.

I didn't trust no one anymore. It seemed everyone who said they cared had an ulterior motive. There were a few people who had said they could help me and promised me the world: nice schools, warm bed, good food, all the good things in life. And then the big king question: *Have you ever had sex for money? Would you have sex for money? You are so cute. Can you sleep in the bed with me?* Walking in on me in the shower. Brushing themselves against me everytime they got the chance. No, I wasn't just paranoid, and when I was I had reason to be. I hate those people, and I will tell you why: they prey on people who are already down and out, or are too young to even know. They use misery as their own source of enjoyment. I never had sex for money and I never gave my body to anyone for anything. I have had some fucked up shit happen in my life that stays where it lies, due to the fact that shit cost me money, drugs and prison time to bury. When I was a kid I made the mistakes kids make, and that haunts me every single day. The dirty fucken dogs, why did they prey on me? Because I was stupid in the way of street living? I wanted to make a friend. Anyone who gave me the time of day I considered a friend. I put myself in situations that let people know I had no one that gave a fuck about me. I told people my life story, minus the shit that happened in my street. I was an easy target. Who could I tell? I was scared of the police because of the crimes I had done to survive. They were the last people I would be running to. I sat for hours crying in the rain across the road from the East Perth Police Station, contemplating going in and asking for help, but each time I got to the curb I'd turn around and walk back. Some nights I would even think of my nice warm bed in Longmore. Even a lock up cell was safer than the streets. I felt like I was a waste of space, dirty, a lost cause. I thought people looked down on me. I thought there was something about me that drew ill-minded people to me. I fucken hated myself. I knew the crime I was doing was wrong but I still did it and in some ways I felt guilty. But I would block that out with drugs or my own hell I was living in.

• • •

I done a lot of things when I was living on the streets and a lot of things happened that I can't talk about in this book. I was angry. Dealing with different people in my life has matured me a lot. I still have a long way to go but I will get there. There are a lot of different things that happened to me on the streets that I haven't dealt with. I blamed different people for different things and looking back now, writing this book, I have put a lot of my past in order. Some things don't look the same as they did back then. Not being clouded by drugs makes a big difference. Some of the things I've tried to write about messed with my head. I don't eat properly. I get snappy towards my family. I don't understand some of the emotions I feel. The pictures I get in my head have a big effect on me and my moods. I am not trained in any form of psychology or anything like that, and I have no idea how the mind works, all I do know is that my mind can fuck me right up. I get all emotional at the silliest things, so if it seems I have more to tell it's because I do and I will when I am stable enough and confident that the drugs are far enough behind me. I won't turn to them. I have my family now. I have to think of them as well.

I was fifteen when I snapped, and I was in Fremantle,

popping pills and taking heroin. I had my first shot of heroin in Perth. I met up with an old Vietnamese friend from Longmore named Pung. He made his cash by dealing on the streets of Perth. Fifty dollar packets of heroin. When he saw me it was like catching up with an old brother, so he said he'd shout me. I'd never had heroin before and I knew it was a dangerous drug. People I had known had dropped dead on that gear in alleyways, in stolen cars, in toilet blocks. They weren't friends, just people I knew of from around the city.

We went to Pung's friends mum's house. She was a prostitute, and no offence, bro, but she was horrid. I don't know how she done it or who she done it with, but whoever, however, they were sick. Sorry love, but you had an impact anyway. She was nodding off in the lounge room chair and she woke up as soon as she heard the door open, like it was business hours or something. As soon as we walked in she was all over my mate and eyeballing me. I got shivers down my spine, and I still do. She wanted another shot as well, offering all kinds of sexual favours to Pung in front of her son. That was some freaky shit in my eyes. Me and the brothers went to the room at the end of the hall, and in that room I was introduced to Madame Heroin.

My life went into a 360° spin the minute the drug entered my bloodstream. I was at peace with the world. Nothing seemed bad anymore. Everything was soft and I was floating. I felt a rush in my throat, and I spewed everywhere. Pung gave the old girl a packet and she cleaned it up and washed my clothes for me. I sat in that room for hours, nodding off into unconsciousness and then waking up to scratch my nose. The shit was a trap, evil in disguise.

My mate shouted me for a week: enough to give me a habit, and that was it. I had found my drug of preference, my bit of paradise. What I really found were lies, deceit, pain, and a roller-coaster ride of ripping people off, selling gear, doing twice as much crime. As my habit grew more and more each day, I was stealing cars, sleeping on the streets, in old houses, down on the beach, anywhere I could. I had a little bunch of people I used to hang around with, all kids in much the same situation as me. We all had different stories to tell, not that we spoke of our lives to each other. We didn't talk about those things at all, just agreed our parents were cunts and that was it.

• • •

One day I met some people in Fremantle at the old gaol. They were older than me and drinking alcohol, laughing and joking around with each other. They asked me for a smoke. I walked over and went to give them one, when one of them asked me if I wanted a drink. I sat down. I was with another street kid, Oogie. He was smaller than me, with stringy long hair. He didn't talk much and that's what I liked about him. I guess I'd been in and out of Longmore a few times by now, and thought of myself as a bit of a hard one. I wasn't the shit, but I thought I was deadly because I could steal cars and I wasn't scared to take a risk. One of the people we sat with had just got some pills on prescription, I think they were cerepax, and a food voucher from the Salvos.

Oogie went missing that day. I bumped into him later in Longmore and he never said nothing about that day. He was just glad to see me. I heard later on in life he ODed on heroin and died. I still don't really know what happened in that house, but I do know something happened. All I can see in my memory is an old house in Fremantle, one of the little townhouses in a backstreet. I remember the kitchen bench, and standing there talking. The house flooded yellow from a yellow light in the ceiling. Then I was in a room, and the door was being held shut by someone on the outside. When I tried to open the door I got flung around the room and rolled onto the floor. I started yelling and that was it. I blacked out with rage. I don't know what I done, all I know is the people from outside ran inside and panicked. I ran straight through the pack of them and out the door. One of them chased me to the door. I was yelling, "Help!" and he stopped. I then yelled, "You cunts are dead! You fucken wait." I punched myself in the face about three times as I was running. And then I was standing in a phone box, ringing my mum, telling her I fucking hated her and every cunt in the world. I was going to kill myself and write a letter telling the world who caused it. Later I went back to the place where I thought all this shit happened and it was an empty block. I drove all around Fremantle looking for the place but I didn't find it. If I did it would have burnt it to the ground with the people in it.

I decided no one else was ever going to hurt me again. I started carrying knives and anything else I could use as a weapon: scissors, empty glass bottles and such. I had had people throw glass bottles at me and they fucken hurt when they hit you.

I just got sick of being society's boxing bag and started hitting back. I did not see the person I was attacking, I could look straight past them. Whoever I was fighting were, as far as I was concerned, my parents, the pricks in my street, my older brother, the dirty pricks who tried to take advantage of me, and anyone else who ever hurt me. Society's answer for me was to lock me up and try to forget me. I lost all respect for anyone else and declared war on anyone who would look down on me and if I thought you were a threat I would get you before you got me. I took any drug I could get my hands on, any chance to escape reality and drift off to where everything seemed all right. I was still scared shitless of everything but I wasn't going to let it hurt me no more, even if it killed me. I threw all emotions out the door, like Skoop told me to do a long time ago.

"An empty machine," he used to say. "Machines don't feel nothing."

"I'm a machine," I'd tell myself. I'd walk around talking to myself, acting out what I was going to say if someone picked me for trouble. But the weird thing was people must have seen me talking to myself and felt the hate I had in my heart, because people avoided me by crossing streets. Dealers who used to give me a hard time didn't even look at me. I didn't see it then but it's a bit clearer now. Before, I looked like a fragile kid trying to act tough. Now, I was a crazy kid who hated everything and everyone and I looked like shit: busted lips, shaved head with a long blond fringe, scratches on my face from something I had walked into. Scabs all over my knuckles from punching shit. I punched everything. Walls, poles, cars, everything. I shadow-boxed in alleyways. The only chance I really had was to pick up a lump of wood if trouble came, but I didn't care. I was training in my own mind.

I walked up to this kid, Robbie, in the main mall of Perth who was standing around six others about our age. Robbie had punched me in the face once at the train station. He knew that butch bitch Donna and thought he would get a name for himself by smashing me in the jaw in front of the whole of Perth train station. Fuck knows how many street kids were there for an audience but I thought I looked like a wuss. It was embarrassing, getting punched to the ground, and to-day was payback day. I saw him standing there smiling, acting all staunch in front of his little group of sheep. I was nervous, I didn't quite know what I was doing, but I was doing it all the same. I was about five feet away and he saw me coming. I saw him look back at one of the girls. Then it must have clicked who I was. But it was too late for him. I king hit him in the head as hard as I could, roaring as I did. People scattered everywhere and left us to it, making a circle around us. But it wasn't needed. That brother just got knocked the fuck out. I busted my hand, but it was worth it. No one said shit. I spat on him, called him a dog, and walked off, shaking like a rattle, spinning out on what I had just done. Everyone was whispering amongst themselves. I wanted to turn around and kick the shit out of him, but I was afraid the police were on their way. The whole mall stopped silent. I went to the train station and jumped on, no ticket. I never had money for a ticket. I'd just jump off when I saw the ticket-officer coming up the carriage.

My life in the city changed a fair bit after that. I had heaps of people come up to me out of the blue and ask, "Are you the one that put Robbie in his hole?" I always made it a point to let them know, "Yes, and it's not over yet." I couldn't think of what else to say. I was a bit nervous, wondering if I had caused more trouble for myself. I was nowhere near the toughest in the city. There were other kids that punched on like men, I was learning, and it was because I was learning and keen and people saw that so most the time they left me alone. I didn't give a fuck no more. If I was scared of you it was on. I hit my problems head on. If I was prepared to slash my own body, tattoo myself, punch myself in the face, call myself all the names anyone else ever called me, what the fuck could anyone else do to me? My head had been punched that many times, they all felt the same. I was numb. I still got a good punch in the head when I went in for a fight, but those punches when you were mad enough to grab someone on the ear and bite it clean off, they didn't feel like nothing. They just fueled the fire.

I wanted to see that big butch bitch on her own without her friends. I would have sorted her right out.

I was still shit scared of her, but that just made me want to solve the problem once and for all. I would have made a big mistake had I caught her at any of those moments, because as silly and immature as I was, I would have cut her head off her shoulders and kicked it around like a football. I didn't see the fact that she had a prick of a life in the past. I didn't know nothing about her, only what she had said in her anger fits at the hostel and when she was sniffing glue. I didn't care what anyone had done to her. I wanted her dead for what she had done to me.

I don't feel the same way anymore. I don't forgive any of them, either. I'm just over it. I pulled through all that shit and plenty of other things I haven't talked about. I took control of a large part of my life through rage and negative walls. Now I am in control of my life. My life was not normal at all, and anytime I did try and live a normal life it was short-lived.

I'd see people with brand new cars, smiles on their faces. I'd imagine their home life and wish I could have their life. I'd see little things like good shoes and nice clothes on people and I'd dream of being able to buy them for myself or walking around a house in my socks, I missed all those little things. I still played them over in my head. The thoughts used to hurt. I'd feel my heart drop.

The thing I really hated was when I'd go to get a food voucher or I'd talk to a counsellor, and they would tell me, I understand how you feel, when they did not know the first thing about how I felt. No one but me and the people who were there when any of this shit happened. And yes, they may have worked similar cases to mine, but they know how they feel, not how I feel. I would much rather them sit down and listen, not try and tell me how to deal with an emotion. I had to deal with the nightmare first. I needed ongoing treatment, not the too-hard basket, or to talk to ten different workers because the first one took stress leave or a better job. I was a kid and that is what was in my mind. I hated seeing other kids with their parents on TV all happy and loving.

That always fucked me off because, as far as I was concerned, that was all false. Really though, I wanted what they had. I was so jealous. I wanted to race motor cross. I wanted to race cars like my old man, and I know I would have been the best at it. I wanted to get haircuts from the hairdressers. I wanted to watch my brother and sisters grow up. Watch videos on the weekends. All that shit was over for me.

You see, I remember that boy so well because he still lives in me. The thing people see is just my work ute I use to get around in and get the job done. I am still me. I always have been me. The people closest to me back then, in those years of my life, were just too blind and ignorant to see it. People who know me now as a father know that I am living a childhood through my children. I am not perfect in anyway. But I am trying to do my best and not make the same mistakes my parents made. I didn't see any of this back then. I went through life, from fourteen up until my late twenties, in and out of prisons, detention centres, and drug rehabs all over Western Australia.

▲ *Ryley and me at his first school—Swan Hill*
Pre-school—for father's day lunch.

BEEN ROBBED

Will he do it no not a chance
Why do you think that coz we wear the pants
Hes tried hes cried the rope snapped he sighed
Why dont you just be done with it
Go on boy you know you wanna quit
Youre not going nowhere any way
Let them all move on to find the better day

Youre just holding off the inevitable
Come burn in hell the heats incredible
Suffer the karma for all of your sins
You played the game that nobody wins
You know who you are
You know what you have done
You done it yourself yes you are the one

You will come to burn with me in hell
Together again isnt that swell
Why lord is there two who control me
Why am I different can somebody tell me
I am one man one body one mind
But if you look inside there is two you will find
I want to cut off my face and slice my throat
Pull my tongue out the slit and start to gloat
Pull off my toe nails nail my toes to the floor
Whos nuts now
Dont fuck with me no more
Cut off a finger stick it in my ear
Im straight you fool who needs the gear
Drugs are just an excuse here help me tie the noose
When I start swinging hang off my legs
Peel my eyelids open with yah wooden fucken pegs
I want to watch the soles jump from my body
I got a right to know who it was that robbed me

Wayne McKay

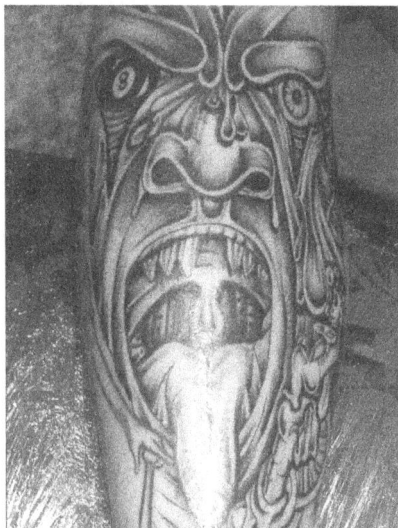

5

DRUG
REHAB

The first drug rehab I went to was Yirra Drug Rehab in Perth. The place was a live-in rehab. I was sent there from court. You had to pay board and do urine tests every week. If you were found dirty you were thrown out of the group and the hostel. Everyone had their own chores, and if they didn't get done, then you didn't get any privileges, like movies, or an outing somewhere such as cable water-skis. They would have been fun events, if the people that were in the place weren't hanging out from whatever drugs they were coming off.

I was getting help for all the drugs I was on: heroin, pills, speed and solvents. I was fifteen years old, not ready to be helped from no rehab either. I had a problem with heroin, a hundred-dollar-a-day problem. I was sick with hot and cold flushes. I could shit through the eye of a needle. I'd wake up in the middle of the night wanting to climb out of my sweat-drenched skin. So I guess I was there for help.

There was a chemist across the road, and one of the other boys in the place was allowed out on day leave. When he came back he was loaded with pills and pot, Advil car-sickness pills, sleeping pills, everything I wasn't supposed to have. The whole place, apart from the workers, got absolutely trashed. The boy that got the pills OD-ed and was rushed to hospital. He was a stringy, lanky-looking kid called Brennox, as silly as they come. I met him later on and learnt a trick or two from him in the way of surviving on the streets.

We all got in trouble at the hostel for breaching our contracts that said we wouldn't take drugs on the premises. Everyone had to sign it when they entered. Some people were there on their last chance from court. If they messed up they were sent to the prison. Two boys got sent back to the prison. One of them was sleeping with one of the drug-rehab workers, so he got a second chance. I ended up leaving because I wasn't getting the help I needed. A week after I left the boy that got a second chance and one of the others, Jacob, took the workers hostage on the activity bus because Jacob was an alcoholic and wanted something to drink. They drove to the drive-through bottle-shop at knife-point, then went on a mad bus drive for around eight hours. He was someone who had been in trouble with the law for bugger all, but entered a rehab filled with criminals to get help. He failed miserably. He turned criminal himself, and I met up with him later on in life in gaol.

There are workers in all those places who do want to

help, but there are also others in there who don't. They are there for a course or a wage. The help is there if you want it, but the place is full of other negative vibes from people who don't really want to be there. They're there to stay out of prison. Those situations never worked for me. I always ended up following the pack and played the help off as a bunch of annoying people who didn't know what they were talking about. I thought they were all text-book psychologists. Each place I went to, I always got on well with one of the workers, but that still didn't make me change my ways. I looked up to anyone who didn't give a fuck, anyone who I thought I wanted to be like. I adopted little bits of each personality I met that I liked, and I created my own don't-give-a-fuck attitude. Anyone I thought was strong enough to have smashed all my problems from my past, I was going to be like that, and the only way to get like that was to fuck up in big bad ways. I thought my life was going to be one big fight, so I prepared myself. I never expected to be a father or have a family of my own. I was going to end up dead. It was just a matter of time.

I think for drug rehab to work there has to be a lot more one-on-one counselling. Group therapy does not work for young people in many cases. I haven't looked at any reports or statistics, I just know from my experience and what I heard from others. If you want help, it's out there. You have to find the right place for you. I found love. That was my cure. Look in the phonebooks, there are plenty of places you can call on toll-free numbers. They didn't help me, but my life is not yours. You could be one of the lucky few who does really get rehabilitated. Ultimately, it comes down to the individual. If they want to be helped they will succeed by helping themself. If there is a bit of doubt in the person's mind, they are not ready in themselves and it's most likely a waste of time. Sad but true.

I stayed at a few people's houses who were probably trying to help me, but I wasn't ready. I was swimming too deep in the shit pit, and for the younger generation just starting to take up the habit you are knocking on the Devil's door. To help them, there has to be a place to put them, like a detention centre, only without the attitudes and the walls. Activities just like the things that kids do. They have to be taken back to their childhood. A farm situation with dormitories, animals to look after, motor-bikes, camping trips, apprenticeships, trades to be taught. A strong artistic section, because nearly every person I know through the system likes some form of artwork. A little recording studio for young hopefuls who want to try and chase a dream. If I had heard of a farm I could go to, where there were fun things to do and where the people cared enough to give me an opportunity to have a life away from the rush of the city, I would have been there in a heartbeat.

There are people working in the system who shouldn't be there. There are plenty of other angels who are trying. It is just bullshit to throw them in rehab and make it look like they are helping, then let the system do the rest. Sending someone who smokes dope to rehab filled with narcotics users, and nine times out of ten they are introduced to the next level of drugs. I don't know about now, but when I was going through that shit, that's what it was like. And it's not like the system has changed a great deal. At the end of the day there could be a million drug rehabs, but if there's no heart to be helped then there's no point.

I notice that a lot of the youth today think it's cool to have people afraid of you and say you're a hard man. But what they don't realise is that for every ounce of me that may look like a hard fucker came five ounces of some fucked up mental pain. There is nothing big about being feared because you are not the baddest person alive. There are people out there who will chew you up and spit you out without a second thought. And if you do have the hard-arse reputation as the tough cunt, you will look stupid when someone completely unexpected takes your title and that's Murphy's Law. People do drastic things when they are scared. Is it really worth bashing people, standing over people, to get what you want in life when it will backfire on you? You succeed while someone else suffers at your hand. If that blows your whistle you're in for a big shock, because at some stage in your life you may wake up and say: *Shit, I've done some bad shit. Why don't people really like me? They fear me, talk behind my back, try to set me up.* Out of sight, out of mind. False friends are all you get when you're in prison.

You'll get a lot more out of life if you put out positive vibes. I can prove that anytime you like. I may not have yachts and lots of high-class shit, but I am happy with what I have. The more good I do, the more good people do for me. Jamie Oliver—I love his work. The world needs a lot more people like him. The people he helps and he gives a chance to would tell you the same.

Not every street kid is going to change, because be-lieve it or not there are the ones who choose to be there. By that I mean, they want to live with no rules in their lives. Not allowed out at night? So run away. Kids that don't want to do as they are told are silly little pricks, if you ask me. Most of them are lucky enough to be al-lowed to go home. By the time they realise that it's not all about being out late at night and having no one to tell you what to do, it's too late. It isn't very often that people who come to the streets leave as the same person. There is always something missing. They've either seen things they shouldn't have, become a victim to other street kids, or picked up a drug habit. All sorts of things are different when you hit the streets. Whether you get taken back home or not, the fact that your parents let you go in the first place is one of the hardest things to deal with, and once it's dealt with and the mental wall goes up it isn't coming back down without a fight. I love my parents, my mum and stepfather, but nothing they ever do will change the way I feel. It's forgiven but not forgotten.

I know I could never have returned home as a kid. I would never have been able to fit in after everything that had happened to me on the streets. I held that against my mum. I had the street attitude and that shit would not fly around Mum and Dad. I probably would have killed my stepfather because I hated him for taking my mum away from me. That is the character who returns home from the streets.

You could be the odd one out and see the error of your ways, have the light shine upon you and shit yourself to the point that you don't go back to the streets. Either way, you are not the same person. It's like letting an animal into the wild: once they get in touch with their killer-instinct, they are wild. The longer they are away, the wilder they get. It may sound like bullshit, but I can pretty much guarantee that any mother out there who has tried to bring their son or daughter home after living on the streets will have had a prick of a time dealing with someone who seems like a stranger in their house. No amount of *sorrys* or gifts will work, not until the kid finds what is wrong and opens up.

I once had this friend, Natasha, who was deaf. She was really pretty with nice long blond hair. She had been raped and bashed nine times in Perth in a space of a year by her ex-boyfriend and his mates. We were very close, but we were just good friends. I didn't know sign language, but I learnt what she meant when she spoke and her girlfriend she always had with her used to tell me. I'd sit with them for hours in the Perth mall, smoking cigarettes and talking shit to someone who couldn't hear me. She always gave me hugs and I loved that. Every time she saw me, she'd yell out and run for me, arms wide for a big hug. She was one of the prettiest girls hanging around the streets and she hugged me. She was another person who killed herself, OD-ing on heroin.

She lived at home with her mum, but she liked the stay-out-late-at-night thing, and got tied up with the wrong people. I hated her ex-boyfriend. He was a junkie-dog. I was a junkie, but he was a dog as well. I can't remember his name, but if he ever reads this book, he'll know who he is and I hope he rots in hell.

FUCK THE TISSUES

I am a man whos seen a lot more than most
A real life horror story but im not here to boast
I walked the circle that had no end
Kept safe behind bars not even the strongest could bend
The paths on coming traffic single file of the putrid
Off to protection where the ill are more suited
Im off to metal work to make myself a shive
Negativity thrives you may have to kill if you want to live
The haunting situation emotions you cant control
You have graduated murder tafe theres a killer in your soul
Tell your story add a few lies
Add soul to your character a demon in disguise

7 oclock wake up the ground hog day rattle
Whos on today three pipers in the battle
Toilet seats lifted floors mopped curtains drawn
Remove filth from your walls zero tolerance for porn
Stand by your doors with shirts tucked in
One step out of line the batten will wipe your grin
Youre a management problem classed out of control
Remove all his clothes and throw him in the hole
One goes by two and then four
An intentional whisper move away from the door
Scream for your mum son no one can hear
Bashed like clock work every week for a year
You are criminals with the label of a screw
I get locked up for doing the things you do

I am the boy that slashed his own wrists
Ive smashed my own face in bare knuckled fists
Sitting in a corner rocking and shaking
What was I thinking was it death I was contemplating?
My skin has been pulled from the inside out
Dish me raw pain and still I wont shout
Now as you can see people ive had some real issues
Theres a tear in my eye poke them out fuck the tissues
Tears dont get back the years

Wayne Hickey

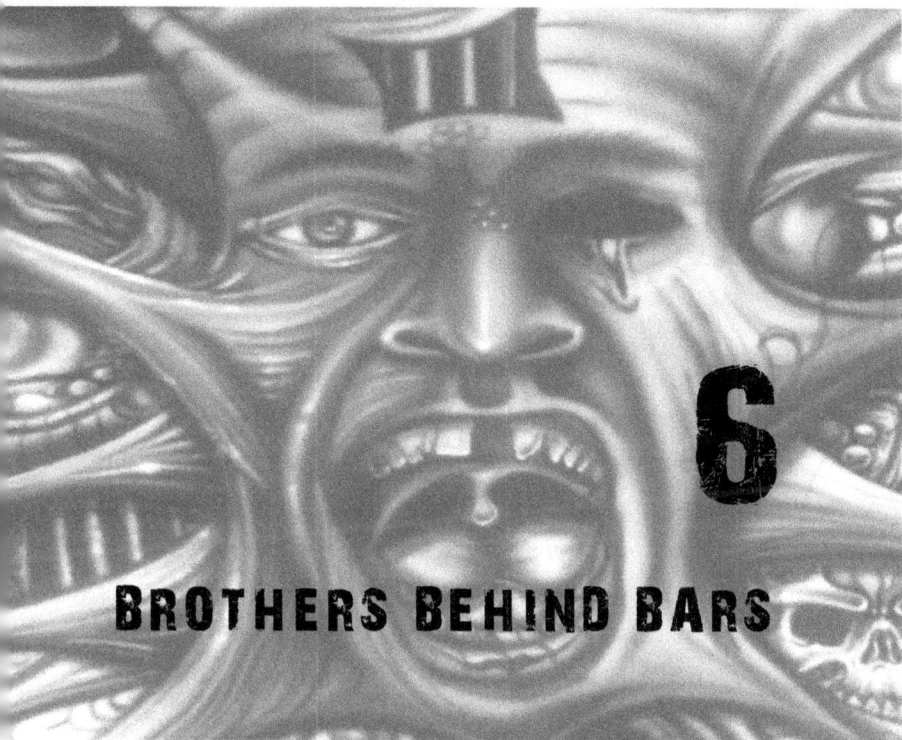

BROTHERS BEHIND BARS

Each time I returned to Longmore things got harder. I was walking around paranoid because people tested me out. Or they would try to start trouble for me so they had some excitement. I seen a boy get his head caved in with a frozen drink bottle, just to find out it was all a mistaken identity. But that's just bullshit. Some bored arsehole didn't like the look of the boy, so he started a rumour that the boy was someone he knew from the outside who apparently ran through this bloke's mum's house. It all came out that it was a load of shit; someone just trying to get a name for themself by bashing people. But Karma plays itself out: I heard that later on down

▲ Air brush, 2007
On canvas a self portrait of me all busted up. It was just a quick painting.

121

the track the same bloke got raped in prison. Not that I agree with that shit.

•   •   •

The second time I went in to Longmore for breaching the order from the first time and stealing more cars. I'm not too sure what other charges there were: damage and burglary, I think. The system gave me a few chances and let me out on more orders, but really I had nowhere to go, so what good were they? I went in and out of the place that many times I lost count. Each time the system hardened me. I got bullied to the point where I was not copping it no more. People would test me to see how far I would go in a bad situation. I was sitting in the classroom on my first day in Riverbank Detention Centre and, like my first day in Longmore, I was nervous. Only this time I knew people from around the place, though not enough to give me a free ride. I had mates, but no one was going to stick up for me. I was different to all of them. If I liked someone I stood staunch and helped out, but I had to earn that shit. I was still fresh.

Riverbank was where the sentenced prisoners went who had been given a fair whack: I had two years and nine months. I was sixteen years old now. I wasn't causing no trouble for myself, but I wasn't copping no shit, either. The classroom was full: about fifteen boys in there, black and white. They had all been there for a while. This boy sitting over in the corner with a bunch of his mates kept staring at me making kissing faces. His name was Dickalo. All his mates were laughing at him doing it. I was getting angry inside. They all thought I was some dickhead. I tried to look away from them but something came over me. Before I knew what I was doing my heart was racing and I had one of the classroom chairs in my hand and ran straight at the prick. All their faces changed from smiles to a sudden shocked look. I swung the chair and just missed.

"Get up, you cunt."

Everyone cleared out of the way, and his mates started egging him on. No one was going for me. The teacher panicked and hit the alarm button.

I looked at him and said, "Come on, you smart cunt. Wanna big-note around? See if I can't knock you out in front of your mates."

He called me a dog and that was it: rage took over. I was no dog. The last bitch that called me a dog tortured me. I was not copping that shit. I launched at him and went flying backwards over the table. On the way through I elbowed one of his mates in the nose—not intentionally. I wasn't even looking at him but shit happens. It knocked his mate onto the floor then suddenly the door burst open and the security officers were all over us. They grabbed me, flung me over onto my stomach and pulled my hands behind my back. I was still yelling at the other boy. The officers were telling me to calm down. I was that angry I was seeing stars flashing in my head. Then they picked me up and carried me down the back, saying to me, "You're gonna be a troublemaker, are you? You wont last long here."

I said, "I don't give a fuck." And at that time I truly didn't.

"Yeah, we'll see about that," one of them said.

I was taken to the punishment cell at the end of the wing and stripped. I had to put on pyjamas. The cell was the same as the one I lived in, but it had no bed mounted to the wall, no mattress, no nothing. Just a toilet, toilet roll and sink. I felt instantly helpless. They could do anything to me in this place and no one would even care. This was the first time I had been in the punishment cells and it wasn't going to be my last.

The other boy was taken to the cell across from mine. As soon as I saw him, I said, "You are fucked, you smart cunt. I don't give a fuck who you are, who you know, or what you've done. You are fucked."

He just laughed at me and said, "I was just joking around with you, brother, and you got all hot over it."

"Yeah, bud, we'll see if you like jokes."

But as the time passed and I realised I wasn't getting out for a while, I started talking to the bloke. I didn't like him, but we spoke for a few hours about the situation at hand. I basically told him I wasn't scared of him or his mates, or anyone else. I was tough. I was scared shitless, but I was at the point where I'd bite, stab, rip eyes out if I had to. I was not getting stood over or looked at like a soft-cock. We were let out that night, back to our own cells, but we had to shake hands first. Like a pair of kindergarten kids. We never had another problem after that. We actually became friends later on in life.

Another time, about five months later, I had trouble with

Willie, one of the Noongar boys. He was in for raping a little girl. I hated the bloke with a passion, because of what he was in for, and also because he did his time way too easy. The day I heard what he was in for I had it in for him, I suppose. I had a little sister and all the shit in my street fucked with my head. He got around acting like he ran the place and I was not copping that shit, even if I did get bashed. I didn't care if he knew I hated him, because I always gave him a dirty look. Then one day out in the yard when visits were on, I walked out of the metal-work room and got pat-searched up against the wall as we did every time. I was waiting for one of my gaol brothers to walk out and Willie walked up in front of the people on visits and in his try-hard gangster voice said, "You got a beef, bruzz? You wanna go? Hey, dog!" That was it for me. I saw red again.

"Dog-cunt! I'll show you dog!" I bitch slapped him as hard as I could. It knocked him off-balance I stepped straight into him, grabbed him by the back of his head with my left hand and smashed my right elbow into his face. Then once again I felt a rush of hands and arms slinging me off. I thought it was his mates kicking the shit out of me and I was fighting to get in control, but I soon realised it was the workers telling me to settle down.

I was frothing at the mouth. I said, "Who's the dog, cunt? Kiddie-fucker. You got bitch-slapped, gangster."

He was all dazed and shocked at what happened. All he could say was, "You're gonna piss, cunt. You're gonna piss."

I rushed back towards him and said, "Yeah, that's right: on your fucken head." All the visitors looked at me like I was a psycho-killer, shaking with adrenaline, spinning out on what had happened. I just smiled at them. All the other boys that were standing around couldn't work me out. This fella had a lot of them bluffed. I didn't care who the fuck he was: I wanted to rip his so-called hard gangster status from him. I didn't want to look like the tough prick, I just didn't want him getting around the way he was. But as many punches in the head that he got he didn't learn shit: he still thought he was the king. It makes me wild today. Willie was taken to the hospital, acting all sooky from that moment on.

My time in detention centres was like a movie. The detention centre set Perth boys against the Carnarvon boys. I had more Noongar mates than I did white fellas. Kingsta was my closest brother, as well as Chrissy—R.I.P. brother. They showed me the ropes. They both loved my artwork as I loved theirs. Chrissy was a brother from school on the outside when we were twelve. But we had different lifestyles. No one liked him when he came to our school, because he was the only Noongar kid in the school. But I liked him because he didn't care what anyone else thought of him. He was a lot like me: no one really liked me, either. We both got in trouble at school a couple of times for smoking, but he left school and got locked up. He had a car accident with Kingsta and killed two people on Christmas night. They went through a red light and crashed into another car. It was in a high speed chase. They were both fourteen years old, I think.

I don't like what they done but, I was doing no different at the time. I just hadn't killed anybody. I feel sorry for the family that was involved. I'd hate to see that happen to anyone. But Kingsta was my family too. He was also a kid and the accident had an effect on him as well. Being a father now myself, I can't even imagine how the surviving family dealt with life after the accident. But I was inside and they were my brothers. They liked me because I stood up for myself, even if I was a bit paranoid at times. They kept me in control a bit. They were boys I wasn't fucking with.

I had no trouble with the Noongar brothers in this place at all. I got on well with them all. Things cruised by when we all got along well. I didn't run the place in any way, and I had my share of trouble. I just did what I had to do. After awhile you build up a bit of respect and a tight crew of mates, and if you had trouble, help was there. I stood up for certain people when they were getting a hard time about something I thought was bullshit. I did it just because that was what my heart told me to do. I didn't like seeing people scared. It seemed like all the white boys and mixes hung around with me and the brothers hung around with Kingsta. Not racially driven or anything, it just went that way. We still were brothers, though. Kingsta was like my brother. So were Big T and Toonie. But we saw this as an opportunity to have some fun. After being in the place for a while a lot of blokes leave or move on to the adult system, and you pretty much get the run of the place. Kingsta had all the Noongars, and all the Kiwis and mixes were with me.

No one got hurt at all, but we had the whole place on tippy-toes: workers panicking, trying to bring us together to sort out what was wrong. But it was too much fun. They could feel tension in the air. We felt it in the air with them. It went on for a week. No one was mixing, when normally the whole place got on well together because any racist pricks got smashed. Most of us were like one big family, but all this spun the workers right out. Every now and then one of the boys would yell out some threat to the other side and the screws would hit panic mode. Me and Kingsta were pulled to the superintendent's office to sort it out. We just laughed at each other about it and shook hands for the man. We were glad it was all over because now we could play basketball together again.

The next day one of my best mates, Hawkins, climbed up the water-tower and took himself hostage. He wanted a helicopter and a pizza, but he got a burst of freezing cold water instead. At three in the morning security officers from the adult system were called in to sort out the problem and they did: they squirted him to bring him down. It worked. He was sent back to Longmore.

As far as me and Willie were concerned, I ended up fighting with Willie throughout most of my sentences. He tried to get me mobbed, and failed. I stood up for myself no matter what, and the time they did mob me it was like getting a massage. Weak pricks. But that was in prison. I may never have got to sort him out the way I would like to have, but he didn't hurt me either, and as an adult now I look back and I'm glad I didn't ever go too far. To the point of killing some one. You'll get stabbed today in prison just for the fuck of it. Over a cigarette.

I done all right. There was a lady worker in Riverbank who I have to say was probably the one person who helped me to believe in myself. Her name was Sandra. She was my social worker. She helped me through a lot of hard times, inspired me to get into my art when I was inside, and helped me get all the art materials I needed. She was honestly an angel, because there were times sitting in that cell where I lost hope and she would do what she could to help me. Even came in on her day off because I got in trouble for something with another worker. She could kind of control me a bit. I didn't like her seeing me wild because she had done so many nice things for me. When I went off my head I went off, but I'd pull my head in like it was my mum or something. The mum I wanted, I think. She helped a lot of other people out over the years. She was respected by the boys and the workers. Some workers didn't like her, though, because she sometimes went against the grain to help the boys out if she could see it would be a positive thing for us. Just little things like a karaoke night, or getting one of the Perth Wild Cats to come in. She did a lot. Thanks, Sandy. You put smiles on a lot of sad faces.

I had some fun times on the inside, even better than a lot of times on the outside. I knew where I stood. No one was going to piss on me, try to fuck me, and if they wanted a fight it was all good because there was nowhere to hide. When you are inside, you sort it out

ASAP and it's done. Get on with your time. No sneaking around shitting yourself. When you seen someone you think was someone from your past, you just run straight into the problem chest-on, arms swinging, and smash until it's all out in the air. If you dragged it on you ended up like me and Willie: at war for years. I suppose it gave me something to do. We both got any shot in on each other we could. He was telling people he was going to stab me in the shower block. Word got back to me so I waited for the next shower call because they could only shower twelve people at a time. And when they let them through the door I was standing there. You can call it dirty, call it what you like but, it was nothing more than a game of who gets who first. I was sick of this knife shit. Stab me, motherfucker, I'll stab myself and laugh at you. I was starting to act like an animal. I didn't give a fuck about nothing no more. I screamed negativity whenever people looked at me, and my self-control got worse. CBS—Can't Be Stopped. I had a self-image to keep. Fuck anyone else if I copped shit.

I am a strong believer in Karma. There are many innocent people who I have hurt trying to keep myself alive, or when I was just being stupid. Karma haunted me. And if I am getting punished for all the things I have done then a lot of other people have some mad suffering ahead of them too. For every punch I have ever thrown I have been hit twice as hard later on in life. So I don't hit people no more. I've seen a lot of ways where I messed up. At least I am trying to help myself. I don't want nothing to happen to me or my family, so I do my best to keep positive, as hard as it may be at times. Believing in Karma helps me to do good things. If I swear at my kids or something silly like that, later I hit my head on something or I kick my toe, and that is no shit: you put out a negative vibe, you get negative back. Every time I have done something wrong when I know it's wrong, I paid for it some way or another. Whether it meant getting caught by the police or something just as fucked up but happening in a different way. Nobody gets a free ride. When people do something wrong to me, I don't even have to lift a finger. They get their own back at sometime. Someone watches over me and I believe it is God. He knows that I am trying as hard as one man can to do the right thing. I'm no angel. I still make mistakes but I'm seeing the mistakes I am making and doing what I can to make sure I don't do it again. I don't really have a problem with what anyone thinks of me for the things I have done. The only people I actually do want to say sorry to are the ones whose chances at living a positive life I may have affected by the fucked-up things I did. Like if I made them a victim of violence, whether it was me robbing their shop or me attacking them because I was angry, or off my face on drugs.

• • •

The way I seen it back then was every single person that I went to for help fucked me over in some way. Whether it was true or not I was too far gone. I had a chip on my shoulder and I was blind to any good around me. They would drop me onto my guts, pull my hands and feet behind my back and use a cable tie. Then they would carry me down the back, always giving me a fucking good kicking too, as soon as we were out of sight. I actually enjoyed getting the shit kicked out of me by the security officers because I loved seeing how angry they got when I laughed. It got to the point where it was regular thing. Me and a mate Trevor, he was a schizo, would wait for Murray to come on, because he was the smartest prick security officer they had. He hated us, because we always gave him a hard time for thinking his shit didn't stink. He brought dirty books into one of the boys and then had his cell searched to try to have him moved to another centre. He was a straight-up dog. He started racial trouble in the place, but we all pretty much knew what he was trying to do. He was Willie's social worker, and he didn't like seeing his boy get tapped in the head. As soon as he would walk into the yard it was on. We would start on him. I'd start barking like a dog under my breath, and my mate would run straight up and dive at him. Murray would wrestle to hit the emergency call button on his belt, and group workers would come running from everywhere. They would dive on my crazy brother. He'd be laughing his head off, yelling, "Weak as piss!" You'd see the elbows get dropped in on his head to try to shut him up, but the more he was hit the more he loved it. I ran over to help and got two steps before I was rugby tackled to the ground, with a knee pushed into the back of my neck and a voice saying, "No, you fucken don't. You stay right there. Got it?" With an extra push of his knee I had all dirt in my mouth.

"Dogs," I said

I was playing it up for my mate. The more I yelled the harder it was for them to control him. I had two officers pinning me down and he was rolling and wrestling around with four others. We both got taken to the choky cells, which means punishment for three to four days, depending if the workers were injured or not. Most of the time they played up and said they were. Not a mark on them, though.

Not all officers were pricks. I'm not saying they were good blokes either, but you got the ones who were just trying to earn their bread and butter. And then you got the ones who had an attitude problem and came to work with the intention of starting shit. Unfortunately for Murray he was one of those, so we loved pissing him off. And that would be excitement for one day. You see most kids played with toys and things. You don't get any of that shit where I come from. You ether played hardball by the killer rule or you became everyone else's means of excitement. By killer rule I mean: it don't matter who, what, when, where, why, or how—you smash. Fuck questions and answers. It's on, no rules style. The dirtier the better. Sure, you can do education and a few other courses but what kid takes that shit seriously when you don't have to? It's all about fighting. Who's the toughest? Everybody gets tested out.

I used to stick up for a lot of the younger boys when they first came in because there were others that would go out of their way to make their time harder than it already was. By making it hard I mean making them feel threatened, afraid of being bashed, or playing the rape card. People do a lot of stupid shit when they are bored inside, such as making fresh people think they are going to get gang-raped. Young punks say stupid shit and if someone doesn't know you and you put that on them, of course they will shit themselves. I know I bloody did. Whether it's a joke or not that's not a nice joke to play. I admit at some stage in my prison life I told someone I didn't like that I was going to fuck them, but by that I meant I was going to fuck them up, not anything sexual.

One thing I could not handle was seeing a reflection of me as a lost little kid in someone else. I would pull them aside and tell them exactly what I had been told when I saw my mate Daniel the first day in Longmore: they weren't in Kansas no more. I hated prisons and the boys homes, but hey, they were home at least. In there I knew where I stood. Some of the boys listened to my advice and some didn't. The ones that listened you never heard a word from, to the point I wasn't even sure they were still in the place. But they were. I seen them from time to time. Sometimes they came and sat with me at morning-tea time. The ones that didn't listen and thought they could get around acting like a big shot had seen too many movies. Those boys either got bashed, put into protection, or just got terrorised their whole sentence. When you saw those boys getting around they looked miserable. I felt sorry for them but they should have listened.

Once you pass a certain point inside you're gone. I wasn't putting myself out for no one that didn't listen.

I didn't get visits or many phone calls. We were allowed

a call a week and I hardly ever used mine, so I was pretty much institutionalised. My family consisted of people on the inside, whether I liked it or not. It grew me into the father I am today and the man I want to be myself.

As much as I hated the system, I do have to say it may have saved my life more than once. When I was too drug-fucked to pull myself out of the shit, no eating for days, weeks even. Or when I'd had enemies I had no chance of standing up against. A quick trip to the joint and I was healthy again, relatively safe, ready for another crack at the title. As the craziest motherfucker on the streets, whether you are aware of it or not, that's all it's about. After you block all emotions and things out, it's a fight to the top. Who's the big boss? We all wanted to be gangsters. Gang, family, it all meant the same thing to me.

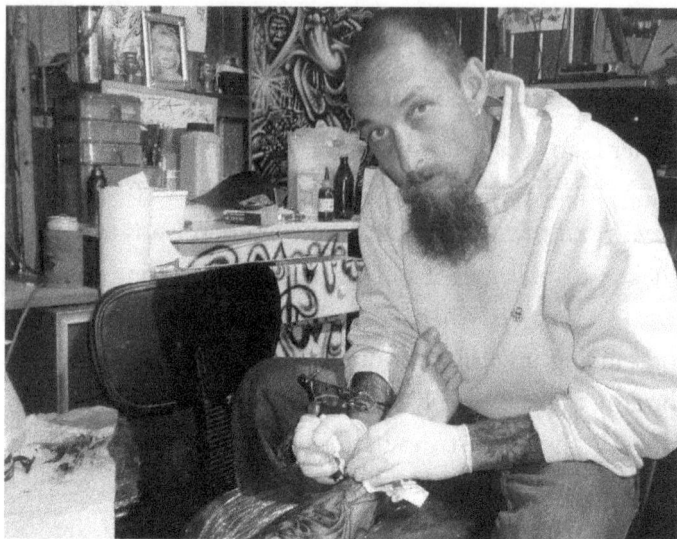

▲ *Me tattooing my brother from another mother—Dan—all freehand work.*

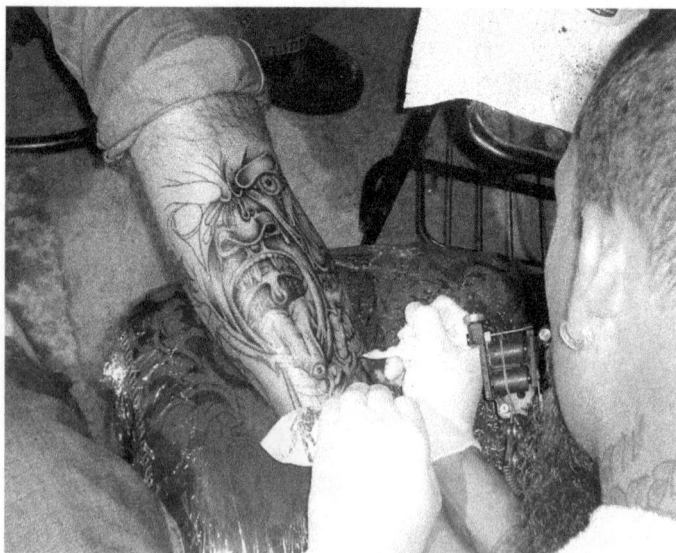

▲ *Me working on Dan's leg tattoo.*

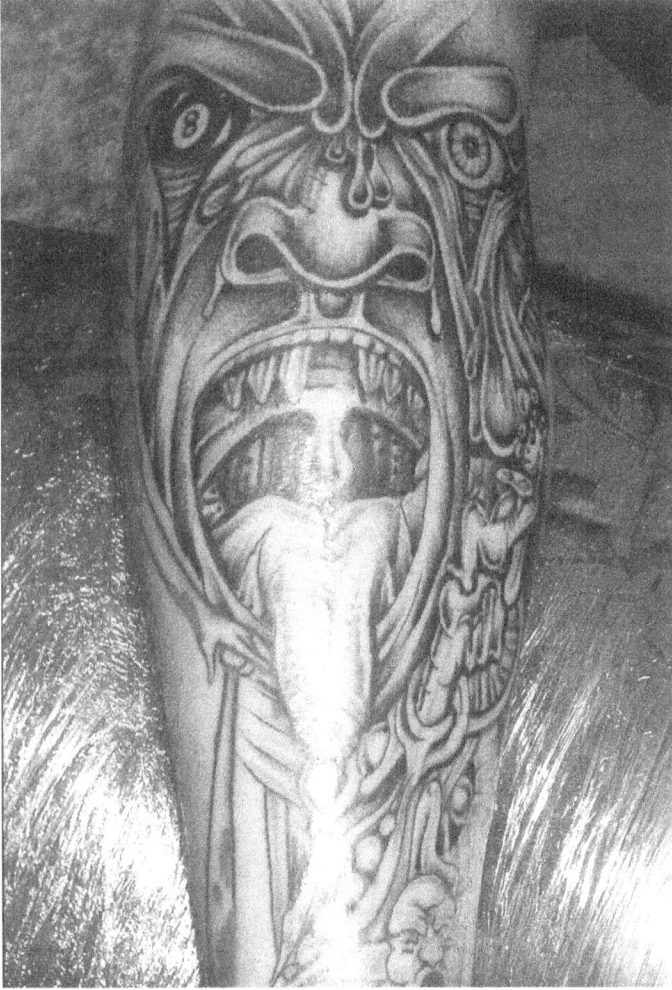

▲ *The end product for the night.*

ATTENTION PLEASE

Attention attention attention please
Everybody here get down on their knees
Do as I say now give me the keys
Nobody enters nobody leaves
Its a hostage situation calling all stations
shoot the suspect no hesitations

I told you I warned you hitch
I said Id be back with the murderous shit
You played me for the fool yeah thats what you get
Paybacks sweet boy aint life a bitch
Custard cut pied merry gut slide
Arms behind the back now we got it zip tied
KillmemanImalreadydeadrunningonlovenowyouhearwhatIsaid
Every day is notch live the double time watch
Fuck with the devil man thats what it costs
Think youre it man you aint shit every one of us the same
Just pig on a spit
Im done with crying no point in lying
bring it on fool get my family high flying
Method to my madness thats what I say
You will know who I was on that very last day

Attention attention attention please
No more locks brother no more keys
paid my dues and I paid my fees
Stand against the wall take a picture say cheese

Youre under arrest put your mind to the test
Lost in the system now rot with the rest
Thought you were the best
Then you fell out the nest look at me now Im the VIP guest
The things that I done I done myself
The lies that I told I told to myself
The ladders I have climbed I climbed with stealth
Im doing it for others not doing it for self
Say what you like dream all you want
Play the game well go the full monty
We only live once one chance at the title
The path that you choose truly is vital

Wayne McKay

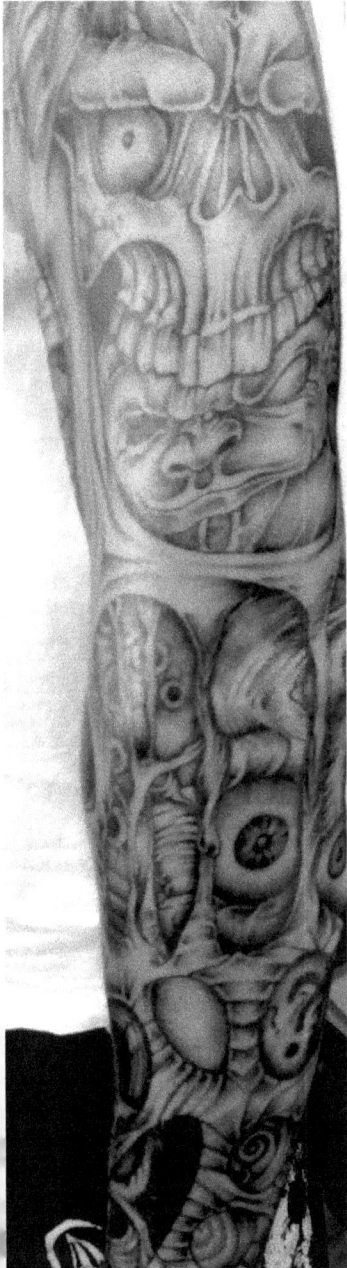

7

THE ADULT
SYSTEM

As an adult on the streets I lived
around Koondoola, Girraween,
Balga—like the KGB Boys. I
wasn't a member, but some of my
brothers from goal were. Things
were different. I wasn't scared no
more. If anything, I wondered
what the fuck was going on
when I was a kid. Being treated
like shit on the streets as a kid
helped me personally not want
to do it myself. That hurt like
hell when I was a kid. I didn't go
out picking on the young crew,
and I'd punch into anyone who
did. To me, whether the young
dude was being a smart arse or
not and there are a lot of little

smart arses out there who think they're all tough, but—truth be known—they get a good slapping.

I was crazy, with a drug habit and prison-time behind me. The way I saw it: if no one in goal scared me, well, no one out here was going to get close, either. I think back now and know I was a bit of a big shot, off my head. I was not paying no fucken junkie for drugs. I made deals. If you dealt drugs, you had two choices: you could say, "Sure, I'll get some in for you," to make yourself think you were still the big man; or you could just give it to me, because if you didn't, no worries, I just had to grab something from a car, and that could be anything from a baseball bat to a tyre lever. The drugs were like petrol to me: if I did not have them I could not run. I sometimes put up to an eight-ball away, and then I would be off. I would feel like I could run through walls for about half an hour, then I would just start looping myself out, running from helicopters that weren't there. If I was walking and someone was walking behind me, I would spin around and start on them. Some of them probably were following me, but they soon changed their mind when they looked into my eyes and saw the lights were on but no one was home. I got to the point were I would just sit there talking to myself, and I would all of a sudden snap out of it and realise there were people around me, listening to me talk, when I didn't even know what I was saying. Talking about frogs and rabbits and things. I was off my head. If I was walking down the street and I saw a car coming, my body would just take off and I would have to follow it, jumping fences and all. I had made the mistake to not run many times in my past, and each time I got the shit kicked out of me. So I thought, *Fuck that shit.* Even if I was bigger and harder, I would not be able to do shit in the state I was in. I would change my clothes in backyards, thinking my other ones were bugged, or just to try to look different. I would hide under cars, in trees, anywhere, until the drugs wore off, or I built up the nerves to move.

I was not born a psycho. I had a pet cat when I was a kid, and I loved it like any normal kid would. Years later, when I lived on my own in a house, I had another pet cat. I would be nice to the cat, but if it ignored me or if it ran I would hunt it down, getting off on chasing it, knowing it was scared of me. I would grab it and scream at it and want to crush its head, but as soon as it looked at me I would drop it and think, *What the fuck am I doing? I'm sorry cat.* The cat would just sit there, freaking out on me. As soon as I put him down again, he would run. Bang! I was off again.

Once, when I had a visitor, we were sitting there talking and I flipped and started chasing this cat around the house. When I caught it, I hissed at it and let it go. It ran out my front door and I followed, over into the bush across the road. I forgot all about my visitor. My cat was not escaping me. Without the cat I had nothing.

I fed the cat really well and kept the kitty litter very clean. I was just obsessed with hunting it.

The visitor left without saying goodbye. I never saw him again.

Actually, he was one of my ex's friends. I am sure

they all had something to talk about. I am used to criticism and smart-arse remarks, and at the time I was honestly off-tap. I really wasn't on the planet and I probably would have cut the bloke's head off if he'd said anything to me.

I am different now. I love all animals. I love saving baby birds, feeding them through drippers. I get really attached to them, and when it is time to let them go, I get pretty emotional. Yes, I know I am off my lemon spread. But hey, no animal ever hurt me. It's people that have hurt me.

I was not always nuts. I adopted that personality somewhere in the shit-heap. But being nuts saved my life as well as fucking it up. Most people who knew me personally say (if they liked me) that I was very straightforward, but the other people would say I was a nasty piece of work. I would just like to say, yes, they are right. But there are also three sides to every story. I just thought I would clear that up with you. If you wonder what I think about me being crazy, I don't like what I did and I advise anyone else like that to get some help.

I want to say this to the brothers in gaol: I ain't no dog. Anyone that's done time with me, my true mates, know that people get jealous and talk shit to try to sink your ship. That's how it is. My views on the system have changed. I am a part of it. You can look at me how you like, but if you know me and you know where I've come from, you know I'm doing this with good in my heart. Call me a dog for walking away, call me whatever you like, but I'd rather be called a dog and know what I'm doing than let some other fuck turn a key on me every night.

I don't like the system, brothers, but I ain't fighting it no more, either. I'm just living my life. I know a lot of you blokes got huge hearts, would do anything for anyone. I know that. We all get fucked up somewhere. It's how we deal with it that counts. I'm no expert. We all know that, and yeah, plenty of blokes and women had it harder than me. I'm just some prick that's done a bit of gaol. I know because I thought the same of Chopper when I first heard of him. But whether we like him or not, writing this book drove me fucken nuts and it was hard work. That man's worked hard.

My peers for a large period of time were murderers, armed robbers, and blokes that just don't give a fuck. I have been accused of crimes: stealing cars, armed robbery, assaults, robbery with violence, grievous bodily harm… and they go on. I have had a good serving from the system, but what about the serving that same system deserves? We all know how I fucked up and I made my apologies. What about the mental mind-games the system plays on people, that keeps us in the circle? Some of us don't want to be in that circle.

I can proudly say I busted out because I saw the system for what it really is: a big money-making plot. Rehabilitation centres they call them. I call them criminal: drug them, mind-fuck them, release them, and see what comes back. Prisons, the hardball players, we all want to figure it out, but no one wants to see the shit half of us can lay on the table, because it's too hard to take in. It's a lot easier to just lock them up and forget them, than to go to a place like Casuarina Prison, or Canningvale, and try fucking with men on the edge. You have to be a dead-set fuckwit: riots and shit don't start over nothing. It's either food, visits, being mistreated by the officers or refusing to give medication to someone who obviously needs it. My message to anyone entering the system is: you either throw all emotions and feelings you once felt out the window or they will be used as weapons against you. Find yourself before you find anyone in prison. We are all one colour inside the walls, and that's green: the colour of the clothes we wear. Stick to yourself, stay out of gaol politics, and hopefully you will be left alone.

• • •

Entering the adult system was a lot different to entering the detention centres. There were a lot more people and these people were hairy-arsed men, to be absolutely honest. I was nervous as all shit. Driving up to the place in the back of a monkey truck was a shock.

I was caught when visiting my best mate while he was in Canningvale: Toonie, a big Maori Brother. It was his first time in the adult system as well. I was on the visit and the prison officers walked up behind me and said, "Are you Mr McKay?"

I looked at them and something inside told me I was screwed. I looked at my mate and said, "I'll catch up with you soon, bruz."

I was walked from the visitor's centre to the reception

and the police came and took me to the Perth lock-up. I had breached my parole again for not reporting in and that was it. I was out committing crime—that's why I couldn't report. I was still on and off the streets when they breached me, so it didn't much matter. But all the same I was nervous as hell.

I was escorted from the lock-up to Casuarina prison, the maximum-security prison they had built in Western Australia when the Fremantle Gaol was closed down. I had heard a lot of things about the place when I was in the juvenile centres, I had even heard about it in the boys' homes. I'd shit myself everytime someone spoke about it. But it was time to bite the bullet: there was no getting out of here.

The first thing I noticed were the shiny coils of razor-wire glistening in the sun. Not just one or two rolls; there were at least sixteen rolls lining the fence line all the way around the prison. It stretched as far as I could see, which wasn't too far because I was looking out two little peepholes in the transport vans they call windows. There were blokes in the van from the courts in Perth, and they reminded me of me, when I was in the boys' home. They were comfortable where they were, at least it looked like that to me. They could tell I was spinning out a bit, because I wasn't saying shit. I was preparing myself on the inside. *No one is touching my arse in this place.* No one is touching me at all. I had plans of sharpening every single thing I could into a point, to put a hole in someone if I had to. I'm not bullshitting. I was scared.

The van stopped and started to reverse. The *beep beep beep* from the reverse alarm was pissing me off. I hated that fucking sound. I'd heard it so many times through my life: at police stations, the mental hospital, everywhere I went that was not where I wanted to be. Always the same fucking *beep beep beep* noise, because I was always in the back of some monkey truck. When the noise stopped I heard the rattle of keys, and voices echoing in the little carport we were in, then another noise. Sounds of the electric roller door closing behind us: that was to make sure none of us attempted to escape, and to be honest the first thing that came to mind was: *I gotta get the fuck out of here.* I considered myself someone who didn't give a fuck about nothing, but really I was somebody who stood staunch in boys' homes. I was not playing little league no more.

The back door on the van opened and there were six officers standing around waiting for us, all in khaki uniforms. There were no soft-touch voices like Riverbank or Longmore. These officers were the real deal. Some had three stripes and some had little silver pips, like the stars you see on a police superintendent's shoulders. All the walls were freshly painted. The place was only about four years old, so it still looked fairly new. There were two waiting rooms in a big reception area. The cells were mainly made of glass. I sat there until I was assessed.

They asked much the same questions as the detention centres, only instead of asking if you were gay, it was, "Are you a poof? Do you take it up the arse?"

Again my answer was no, but I pretty much told the

officer to get fucked. My nervous mouth couldn't control itself. I said, "Nobody's fucking me, mate."

The officer sitting in front of me typing on his computer stopped dead and just looked at me. I saw his silvery hair covering his forehead slightly lift, so I had a clear view of his eyes. He had a look on his face that said, *I have heard that before.* A slight smile came to his face and he just went back to what he was doing.

"Do you have any enemies or anyone that has a problem with you in this place?"

I looked at him and said, "How would I know? I haven't even been in there yet."

"Do you want protection?"

Now that question spun me out a bit. I had heard of protection, and people that put themselves in protection were all classed as dogs. That's what gets around the detention centres. And I was not being called a dog by no one. I know all about how that shit works. Dog in the same sentence as your name means you're everybody's excitement. And everyone is your enemy.

I looked at him and said, "No protection."

Whether I had enemies or not, it was too late now, and I'd much rather have gotten bashed in the mainstream than be known as a dog in protection. I don't believe everyone that goes to protection is a dog. Some people just don't have gaol in them and are not from our lifestyle. They make one mistake and end up in a place that they only ever had nightmares about. Protection is filled with paedophiles: we called them *tamps, dogs, rock spiders, kiddie-fuckers, filth,* plus many more names.

Whatever springs to mind. They get put there because they are at threat of becoming a victim of violence. Most of them choose to go there. Some think they can handle the mainstream and go under cover, but most of the time they end up bashed or stabbed and then sent to protection anyway.

Unfortunately there are a few of them that get around like their shit don't stink. It's because of who they are: carrying a certain last name gives you certain rights. That's bullshit, though. What's good for the gander's good for the geese, I say.

Other people use protection. You have the people up there that get drugs in the system on credit and can't pay. So they turn to the screws (that's the prison officers) and either give the person up who's after them, or they make up some bullshit so they don't give the other person up. Either way they are still seen as dogs by the other inmates. Or there are the ones who have been flogged for no reason in particular and can't handle the pressure. And then there are people who are paranoid of the prison. Protection has all types in it. There are still a lot of people in mainstream that should be in protection, and I don't say that for their own good. I say that because that is were they belong.

◀ Air brush, tin
This is the top left corner of a much larger painting.

I have different feelings towards the whole prison system, now but back then, when I was still thinking I was mature and fresh myself, I went along with what everyone else was doing.

After the officer finished asking me questions he told me to go back and sit in a little room. About two minutes later another officer, Mr Carrol, came over to the door and opened it. Again I heard, "Follow me." He walked over to the corner of the room and told me to stand against the wall. There were numbers all up the wall for measuring your height. I was told to face him and he handed me a little magnetic board with my name and my date of birth on it. "Hold that under your chin," he said, "and look at the camera." Then *flash!* It was done.

I was told to walk to another room. This was a shower room, similar to the one at Longmore and Riverbank, only it didn't smell so mouldy. They weren't used too much by the looks of them. My clothes were all in there, hanging on the wall in a white laundry bag. An old man in a green tracksuit walked in the room. He was about fifty, with coke-bottle glasses. He was a prisoner as well, but he worked in the administration, getting all the clothes for the new inmates that came in. I spun out on him at first, because he was the oldest looking prisoner I had ever seen, and he looked like a suspect of some putrid shit. He sure wasn't in for robbing banks and stealing cars. I felt uneasy around him for some reason, but that was just the way I was. I didn't trust anybody, especially no old dudes that was working with the screws. I had an attitude against any of that sort of shit.

The old man came over and gave me a little plastic card with my photo on it, and my name, date of birth, and the name of the prison, as well as Ministry of Justice. He told me to wear it at all times.

He said, "Try your clothes on when you get back to your cell. If they don't fit, put in a white form and I'll call you down on Monday to change them."

I looked at the bag of clothes and prayed that they were all my size. The fella disappeared out of the room and all of a sudden an officer walked in with another bag in his right hand. It had hard objects in it. I could see the outline of a dinner plate. The red plastic was just visible through the material. The bag was full. It had my sheets, toothbrush, shaver, knife, fork, spoon, a plastic cup and a bowl. There was a piece of paper inside with a list of items on it and a price for each item. If you damaged any of the property it had a cost: a plastic bowl was three dollars. A cup was worth one dollar. The cutlery was worth eighty cents each. Even your sheets had a price. Everything was at your cost if it was damaged or lost. I had two white towels as well.

The officer told me to strip off and put my clothes on the bench. He then started searching them. After that was done he asked me to: *turn around, squat, cough, stand up, lift your right foot, wiggle your toes, lift your left foot, wiggle your toes, spread your cheeks, bend over, stand up, turn around, face me, lift your balls, hands in the air, wiggle your fingers, open your mouth, lift your tongue, run your fingers through your hair.* I was used to doing these things, except bending over with my cheeks apart. I felt strange and uncomfortable doing that.

As soon as we finished I was told to have a shower.

I asked, "How long do I have, boss?"

He replied, "Two minutes."

I grabbed one of the towels off the bench and carried it over my shoulder to the shower. There was a hot and a cold tap. That was a change. There were no taps where I had been before: the workers controlled the water. I turned the shower on and stepped under the water. I shut my eyes and imagined I was in a shower in a house on the outside. It didn't even feel like two minutes and he yelled, "That's it! Time's up!"

I turned the taps off and got dressed. The clothes included a brand new, prison-issue, prison-made tracksuit. I put the thongs that were in the bag on and I was ready to move. I felt like a frog with white feet.

I was then taken to the medical centre. We walked through a number of doors. They all had electric locks. Everything seemed like space-aged shit. It was an arty-looking prison. The bars on the windows went across-ways instead of up and down. They looked like I could almost fit my head through them. I was wrong, though. The walk to the medical centre was down a long foot-path in the main yard. When I walked through the doors to enter the yard I had thought they would lead us to the medic's office or something, but instead they were the entrance to what seemed, at first glance, like a big retirement home. The place was huge: footpaths lead-ing everywhere, green grass neatly cut. There were nice gardens all over the place with flowers in full bloom. At the end of each pathway there was a cell unit with four wings, holding approximately sixty prisoners a side. The place as I seen it was very well looked after. The inmates obviously worked hard here.

I heard people yelling out from windows. I couldn't make out what they were saying. I was too busy spinning out on the size of the place. Without a lie I would say it was about the size of six full-size football stadiums. There were tennis courts and basketball courts at each unit. I asked the officer which unit I was going to and he said, "You'll be in the admin unit, cell block five, on the AC side for about one week, just for assessment. Then you'll be placed into one of the permanent cell blocks."

I asked what AC meant and he replied, "There is an AC side and a BD side. In five block, BD is protection." I panicked because I didn't hear what he had said properly.

"I'm not going to protection."

"I didn't say you were," replied the officer instantly. I felt a sigh of relief come out of me.

Boss pointed to the cell-block, second last from the end on my left hand side, and said, "That's where you are going. If you behave yourself you could be out of there in a couple of days. If you're a smart-arse you will be there for longer. As well as assessments, there are also close-supervision prisoners in there who have come out from the punishment cells. That's where you start from scratch if you get in the shit. There's a lot of trouble-makers in five block."

I thought to myself, *Oh fuck. Gee thanks, straight to*

the fucken nutters. I'm definitely going to get killed in this place. I had an attitude, and my ways were: go in hard or don't go in at all. The lifers called my type trouble. I didn't want to be trouble. I just didn't want to be seen as anybody's bitch, either. I was a frightened man that was capable of making big mistakes in little China if I had to. That was what I told myself. Telling myself that made me think I was ready for whatever would come.

After walking for a few minutes we came to a little building. On the door was the sign that said Clinic. This was the last stop before I was put into my new home. I had the standard check up. Was I on any medication they needed to know about? Did I have AIDS, Hep, Hep B?

I answered, "No to all of the above." I was clean of diseases. I'd had a blood test in Riverbank but I still got another one, and they weren't gentle about it either. I weighed in at 68 kilos: skin and bones. Just a junkie piece of shit. I'm not being hard on myself, that's exactly what I was. But I was about to get healthy. The doctor gave me a couple of tablets to make me sleep better because I was coming down off speed and whatever other pills I was on at that time. I was made to take the tablets right there and then and had to open my mouth and lift my tongue again. Once they were happy that I had not stashed my pills for later it was time for me to enter the game.

We walked up the little pathway to unit five. The place was alive inside. Everything was quiet outside be-cause everyone had returned to their units. I think the silence before kind of threw me off. I looked through the glass doors, hoping I'd see Kingsta or one of my brothers from the juvie centres, but there were no familiar faces. The door beeped and boss pushed it open. We walked in and there was a downstairs and an upstairs landing. We walked upstairs. C-wing. I was C3. I could see the numbers on the top of the doors. My cell was the third one up on the left. I walked in and put my bags on the top shelf in the cell. The officer walked in and pushed the call button at the end of the cell. About one minute later someone answered. "Yup?"

"McKay in-house."

"Yup." The speaker turned off.

The officer then handed me a key and said, "You are two out with an old-timer. Bit of luck you will be out in the main blocks soon. "Then he turned and left me. He stopped at the door and said, "Listen for your name to be called over the loudspeaker. When you hear it, go to the control room in the end of the wing."

I said, "Yeah, boss," and he walked off. I was alone for my first time in the big house, the concrete jungle, big Casablanca. The place that I had heard nightmares about: rapes, murders, bashings, rumours of prison officers hanging prisoners in the middle of the night, mobbings from the prison officers.

• • •

Certain guards formed a gang, but I make no further comment due to the fact that, enemy or foe, I ain't no dog. I've been an SK South Style gang member. We may have only been a prison gang, but it got us through. I

have a fair idea how a gang works and the whole system
works as we do. They had spies, we had spies. They had
weapons, we had weapons. They had higher-ranking officers, we had higher-level brothers. They used tactics
and we used tactics. If one of them got bashed, they
mobbed us. If one of us got bashed, we mobbed the officers. The difference was: they got to go home. We stayed
in prison. They wore uniforms, we wore tracksuits. What
we did was illegal. What they did was legal. Still, both
were gangs. Our ways may have been more confronting
but that was because we didn't have little hidden cells
that we could pull someone into and flog the shit out of
them. I've never been in no highly organised gang but
I've been in crews that stood staunch by each other. I
can't say any more on that due to the fact that I have respect for my brothers still choosing to live the lifestyle.

My participation as a member was nothing to be big-
noting about. Until I found my place I was just another
green bit of clothing. My number was 940018 and that's
all. I was just a number.

● ● ●

The cells were nothing like the shape of the juvie cells.
There were three long benches running up the side wall,
two plastic chairs, two bunk beds up the other wall, a
toilet with a concrete divider so you had a little bit of
privacy. I spun out because we were allowed to take our
knives and forks to our cells. It also made me nervous
in a way because there were some mad-looking broth-

ers in this place. If my cutlery was seen as damaged I'd get charged. But if I was damaged then I was damaged. I decided I'd take my chances with the charge. *As soon as I get a chance I'll sharpen something up,* I thought.

I could feel tension in the air; people calling other people dogs. Just hearing that word you know there is going to be trouble if the bloke has any dash at all. But to my surprise nothing happened. One of the fellas was black, the other was white. I was staying clean out of it. I thought to myself, *What the fuck would I do in that situation?* All I knew was that I wasn't copping that shit. I walked back into my cell and shut the door. I was nervous as hell. I picked up the half-used roll of toilet paper and ripped a bit off about two foot long, folding it in half once. Then I grabbed the toothpaste off the sink and put two little dabs at the top of the little square window in the middle of the door. I pushed the toilet paper up against the toothpaste so it blocked the view if anyone looked in. Then I walked to the top shelf and picked up my pillowcase. I took my new toothbrush out of its plastic case and started sharpening it on the concrete divider between the toilet and the bottom bunk bed. I was shaking like a leaf, thinking if I got caught by a screw or a crim I was fucked. I'd be charged by the prison for possessing a dangerous weapon and intent for some ill-shit. I wanted the thing sharp and I was not stopping until it was. My hand was going like lightning. One side was done. I rolled it in my fingers and started the other side. I took a bit more care: I wanted it to be right, just in case. It took me about ten minutes until I had something that had the potential to be a deadly weapon. I put one of my jumpers on the mattress and thrust the toothbrush into it. A little pop and it was through and into the mattress. I was set. I instantly felt a little more at ease. I put it down the front of my pants just above my groin. Easy access if it was needed. Not that I wanted to use it, but I have to be honest, there were thoughts of wanting to test it just to make sure.

There were a couple of people I was paranoid of already. Not that I had done anything, just that I was tall and my fucking face must have said, *Have a go.* My look had gotten me into trouble in the past. There were fellas everywhere walking in and out of cells, people were sticking their heads out to see who the new face was. Every single one made eye contact. I was not looking away from no one. Look at me—I'm looking at you. Some of the eyes I seen were the scariest eyes I've ever seen. I didn't know none of these people from a bar of soap. I had seen a couple of blokes with a few dodgy tattoos in my time, but some of these dudes had the shit all over them. Their faces were completely covered.

One bloke had *dog* tattooed on his forehead, and he cut his ears off long before Chopper thought to. This fella even cut his dick off and handed it to a female prison officer. He was a big dude, too. I looked at some of these people and thought to myself, *I'd better brace myself. This don't look too good.* I thought I'd be able to handle myself if need be, but the reality was if I was caught unawares at any time I wouldn't have a chance. These blokes were just as bad as me, some were a whole lot worse.

In reality I was an L-plater.

The first thing I done was go looking for a cigarette. There was a bloke waiting to use the phone holding a packet of smokes. He saw me coming and he knew exactly what I was looking for.

I said, "Hey, bro, any chance of grabbing a smoke off you? I'm new here and I haven't got shit." The fella was not the everyday looking gaol-bird; he was not really a hard-looking man. He was a speed cook that got busted in the act. It was his first time in trouble with the law. Well, that's what he told me, anyway. I never really got to know him too well. He gave me a smoke and told me to go and get a packet of Winni Red off the screws. I looked at him like he was trying to fuck with my head or something.

He said, "Nah, I'm serious, bro. You get an entry packet if you're a smoker. They take the money out of your gratuities next week." I asked where I had to go to get them and he pointed to the fish-tank looking thing in the middle of the whole unit.

There were about five officers sitting in there. They were laughing at something. One of them saw me coming. He had three pips on his uniform. He would have been in his late forties and looked like an arsehole. About five foot, a solid build, balding on top, and a big fat beer gut. He looked like he had been in the business for a while. He opened the sliding door saying, "You're McKay?"

"Yeh."

The officer looked at me and said, "Yes, what?"

I looked at him and thought to myself, *What the fuck?*

"Oh, yes boss," I said quickly.

"Come with me." The door to the side *beeped*.

Boss said, "Push it." I pushed the door and walked through. He took me into a little office and said, "I'm Mr Carr. You'll call me boss or sir. I'm the SO in this unit at the moment and that means I'm in charge. Have you ever been to prison before, or locked up?"

I said, "Yes. Not prison, though. Just training centres, boss. Longmore and Riverbank." Just as I finished saying that there was a knock at the door another officer walked in holding a yellow file. It had my name on it, as well as a whole shitload of paper-work inside it. It was my juvenile history. The officer that walked in was only a rookie. He was young and he didn't even have a pip or a stripe. He was not much older than I was by the looks of him. He handed the file to the SO and walked out. The SO opened my file and skimmed through, reading a couple of sections.

He said, "You gonna try to kill yourself here, are you?"

I said, "No. That was a long time ago."

He looked back at my file, skimming through a bit more. He stopped and said, "Had a bit of trouble from you in the boys' homes from the looks of this. We don't like smart cunts in this place. This place isn't for kid-brain cunts, either. You think you're tough, son? You will get chewed up and spat out in this place so fast you will wish you were never born."

I gulped to myself, thinking, *So what the fuck am I supposed to do? Be a mute? Sit in my cell all day and not come out? Or what?* People pick you in gaol for no reason other than boredom half the time. I knew that from experience in the boys' home. There were a lot more people in the prison than there were in the boys' home and I wondered if Willie was in prison yet or if Boy Roe—another fighting mate—was here. They were in the Bird Killer Gang together. Don't ask me where they both got that gang name from, but that was their crew when they were in Riverbank.

I had all sorts of things going through my head. I had to get to our crew to adapt to this shit.

I asked the SO, "Is Kingsley Pickett here, boss?"

The SO looked at me and said, "Do you know Kingsley, do you?"

"Yes, he's a brother, boss."

"So you're a gangster, are you?"

I looked at him and said, "Nah, boss, just brothers from when we was young. I don't know no one else here, that's all."

"I'm pretty sure you'll know a few more of the lads in here when you get out there, you'll see." He gave me a packet of smokes (White Ox), rollies and a packet of Tally-Ho papers.

"You smoke?"

"Yes."

"Then make those last till next week, 'cos you won't be getting no more. We take the price of these out of your wages at the end of the week. If you're unemployed you get twelve dollars a week, level five."

The highest wage we could get was forty dollars a week, but that was for level one workers. Canteen spends were on Wednesday. The max we were allowed to spend was thirty out of our gratuities and forty out of our private cash, which is an account that visitors can put money into. On the weekends we were allowed two hours of visits. You could have one hour on each day or two hours on the one day. It depended on how full the visitor's centre was at the time. I was told if anyone wanted to visit they have to book in advance by one week. They were not allowed to bring anything in and if you wanted to have money in your account they also had to apply to do that if it was more than the fifty dollar a week limit. People could put money in for you to buy a TV, but you had to apply for that too. The TV was bought from the prison canteen. That was if you were lucky enough to have someone that gave enough of a fuck about you to do any of those things. I had a few visits here and there but they were from an ex from hell who just done my head in. But that's another story.

The SO said, "Do you have any people whose phone numbers you want to put down on your phone account?"

There was a form for inmate phone calls. There was enough room for eight phone numbers.

To make phone calls you had to buy little orange or blue tickets from the canteen. They cost forty cents each, and to use one you had to go to the wing office in your cell block and ask an officer for a call. You gave him the ticket and he ripped it up and threw it away into a special bin they had. The officer would then tell you to go to the phone in the bubble hanging on the wall right next to the screw's box, the fish tank, whatever you want to call it. I'd have to tell him who I wanted to ring so he could put the number through. The reason we had to have a phone list was so the prison could ring and get permission from the people you wanted to call. The idea was that nobody could call people and harass them. The call time limit was programmed into the phone and it cut out after ten minutes exactly. The phone would beep every ten seconds for the final thirty seconds of the phone call. At the beginning of the phone call there was a recorded message that said: "You are about to receive a phone call from a prisoner at Casuarina prison. Do you wish to receive the call? If you do not wish to receive the call hang up now. Go ahead please. "Your ten minutes started from there.

I learnt fast that there were heaps of dramas over the phone. Every night there was a queue for the phone about ten people long. There was not even enough time to fit in ten people before lock up at seven o'clock.

We were let in the unit at four-thirty in the afternoon. Tea and everything had to be done in that time. So as you could imagine, plenty of trouble came from the phones. I had a problem with Alan Bond. He didn't like me and neither did his big dopey bodyguard Ian Jeffries. All because of the phone. But that was during a different sentence.

I got the run-through on the prison rules: no fighting, bullies are not your friends, telling is not dobbing, don't be afraid to approach a screw. *Yeah right.* That is a load of bullshit if I ever heard one in my life.

The truth of the matter is if you were seen talking to the screws you were suspected of giving information on who was bringing drugs into the prison or other gaol political bullshit. If you gave someone up for anything you were a dog. That's that.

Some officers were there to do their job and just the same as everywhere else there were those who were getting some kind of revenge on the inmates. Maybe they had their lunch taken off them at school or their women left them for a bad boy—who knows?

Prison is a place full of mind games. I learnt that in my first few days. I got a harder time from the screws just trying to find my place than I did from the crims. Sure, I had people making me paranoid, making me think, *What the fuck was going to happen to me?* But I also made up my mind that I would deal with any problems fast and hard. The problems from the uniforms were a whole different issue. They got away with whatever they liked.

The little things in gaol are really the big things. When you have nothing they pass you off to each other. One officer would say one thing, then another would do the complete opposite. If you really needed a phone call to someone on the outside because the inside was toying with your mind, or you asked to see a psych, they'd say "Yes" and nothing would get done. You'd put in white forms to be interviewed for a job or something, and every attempt you made went missing. The screws would call you a dog, no second thought, but do it back and see what happened. If that was rehabilitation, yeah, doing a great job. Holding off on medication for people they knew needed it. At night time you could just rot in your cell. Don't go getting crook and pushing the call button for assistance, because in all honesty, unless your arm had fallen off or your cell was on fire, they weren't coming. If you pissed the officers off just once, you were fucked. They made you look stupid in front of the other inmates just by saying shit out loud so the other crims could hear.

Shit like, "Don't come sooking around here for phone calls. This ain't a holiday."

I wasn't sooking. I asked to ring my lawyer. As far as I knew we were allowed to ring our lawyer at any time during the day.

If the officers were giving out the fruit at meal time, they gave everyone else theirs and missed me out. Letters that I know had been sent, letters with photos of my brother and sister, went missing. You don't get much in gaol if you don't have much and what you do get means a hell of a lot. I found prison officers played mental games to try sending inmates out of their heads. In all honesty half of them should be in prison themselves, because we get punished for the shit we do whether it's for surviving or just being criminal. They do it to anyone who enters a prison. And they are trusted to help rehabilitate. More like help to inject a known fate. There are no releases for anger and frustration in prison, unless you want to punch a boxing bag. But that's just training for what you want to do to the person fucking you off. The anger and rage you get dished in prison stays with you when you are out of there. And no bullshit, I believe that adds to the crime rate as well.

You can go to a prison a gentle-souled man and come out a man with a temper bad enough to seriously hurt someone. Don't think that I'm saying I feel sorry for the prisoners because I'm not. We need prisons, there is no doubt about it. But the workers should be better trained to deal with their own emotions before they go to work with either straight-out criminals or mentally unstable people. You see movies with prison officers taking cash and all that kind of shit—it really happens. It's just not as open. Not all officers, of course, but a large number are criminals themselves.

There was an officer caught bringing in drugs to Canningvale while I was there, and the same in Acacia Prison. They lost their jobs and got a fine, saying they were made to bring it in. That is bullshit. The truth to the whole thing was the officer saw a dollar sign and took advantage of a situation. There are bashings in prisons all the time from prisoners and officers. An officer will get a punch in the head for playing mind games, like booking a visit when no one even booked, or hanging up on a phone call halfway through when an inmate is upset on the phone. Everything, any little thing, that will get a bite out of an inmate is done, just to provoke a reaction. Sure it's learning to deal with life's stresses. But when you are in a cage that's not a normal life. If you don't want none of that to happen to you, stay out of trouble. And don't get wrongly convicted—innocent or not you will still get plugged by the system.

• • •

The meal times were the same as in the detention centres: breakfast as soon as they unlocked at seven in the morning, lunch at twelve, dinner at five-thirty. All the meals were shit, either burnt or not cooked properly. The best meal in the place was brekkie because you made it yourself. Toast or cereal. There was a toaster in the mess hall at the end of each wing, and the cereals were in a cupboard that got unlocked the same time as they unlocked us. The cupboard was locked again at the morning muster.

Then it was cell cleaning. Toilets cleaned, seats lifted, curtains drawn, floors mopped. No porn posters on the wall, meaning no breasts, no below the waist pictures, no pictures on the wall period. Clothes folded and in the cupboard.

At eight o'clock it was morning muster. Stand by your doors, t-shirts tucked in, name tags on. Name tags to be worn at all times. There were seven musters a day. For each one you stood by your cell doors, unless you were at work where the muster was done by sight.

My first night in the place was probably the night I remember the clearest. I was put in a cell with an old gaolbird who had some stories to tell. I say this because I think I heard every single one of them over a three-day span. As soon as lock up came he introduced himself to me as Johnny Fry from Sydney. He said he was an old gangster and no doubt he was, back in his hey-day. He was a fit looking old man, five foot four, and had obviously trained a bit over the years. He had been accused of murder a few times but I never got the full story from him. To him it was just, *Yeah, I knocked Stevie Black and I knocked Bobby Boob, but they were dogs.* He said he'd done thirty years for that all up.

Hearing all this shit was spinning me out. I'd met some bad men in my time. At least, I thought I had, but I didn't know shit. Whether what the fella said was true or not, he had me spinning out and he knew it.

He made little jokes like, "If you get cold jump down here with me."

I looked at him and said, "Look, bud, no one's fucken cuddling in this cell. I'm not into that shit." My heartbeat dropped out of my arse. So much shit was going through my head it was not funny. I was thinking of jumping down of the bunk and stabbing the fella in the neck. I only had to do eighteen months. *Was it worth doing life over? Was I going to let this fella fuck me?*

Johnny must have felt my vibe, because he said, "Jump down brother you're right mate I'm no queer. I fucked a few blokes that were though."

I spun on him then he said, "Nah, not doing long enough this time to be poofing it. But I'm open to suggestions."

I saw he was playing with my head so I laughed at him. "They might find you all bunged up in the morning old boy." I realised what I had said and thought to myself, I hope he didn't take that the wrong way.

But he didn't. We were cool. He had some cards, and even though I didn't play cards I played a couple of games. I don't remember what we played. I was pretty bombed from the medication plus a bit strung out from the gear. He played head-fuck games a lot, but he also taught me a few things. Throughout my gaol time he had rorts everywhere because he knew everyone. It was probably lucky for me that I didn't stab him. I'd have been fucked in more ways than one.

I was moved to 2 Block within three days, where my gaol time started. There where some good brothers in that wing, including my brother Kingsta, Big Brad, one big boy Greg Quartermane. Greg may have been a hard-core criminal on the outside, but when he was in gaol anyone who knew him knew he was a gentleman. R.I.P. Greg. Little Brad

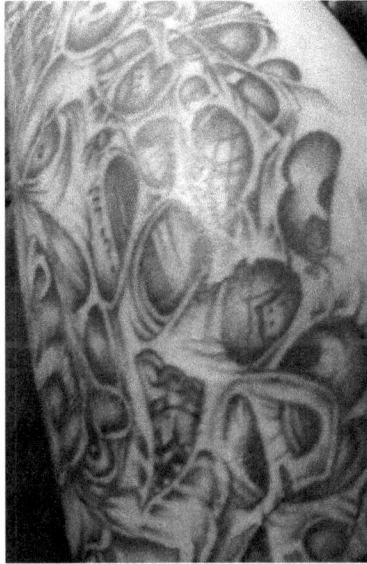

▲ *A leg tattoo done on Darren in Swan Hill. A mad fan and good friend of mine. If you look closely you can see the making of the words RAW DEAL. It's all freehand.*

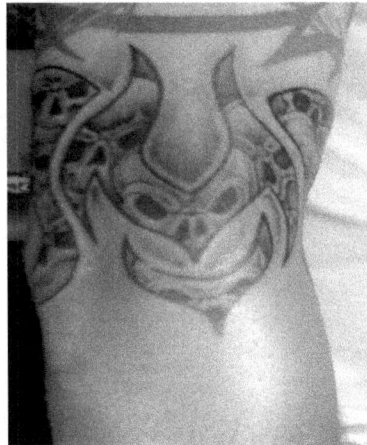

▲ *Negative tribal on a friend of mine*

169

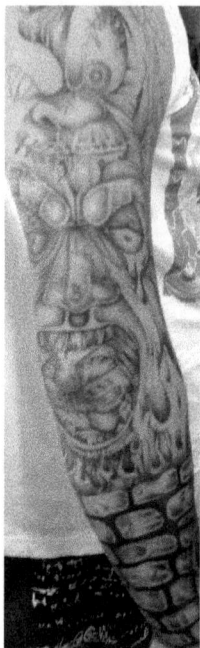

▲ *L.M.B Brother Boras freehand tattoo that I done over 200 hours with a 7 needle round shader.*

and Marty two other brothers that had done ten years, were actually blood brothers. Little Brad made my time hard at the start. He had to test me out, I think, to see if I would stick up for myself, and he learnt that I would. But that is another story all together.

• • •

Within my first week in the place I knew everyone in the wing. The older brothers had a bit of time for me because they saw my artwork, and Kingsta's uncle, a tattooist, was in the wing. I wanted to learn how it was done. He taught me how to make a gaol machine and ink for it out of soot from an oxy-acetylene flame in the metal workshop, and needles out of guitar strings. All I needed was a tape-recorder motor or a cd player motor, a toothbrush, Artline pen, the inside ink tubing from a biro, a staple, and a clock radio to run it. First, cut the brush part off the toothbrush. Heat the toothbrush up about an inch down and bend it so it looks like the letter L. Get the little round motor and sticky tape it to the short part of the L. The little steel shaft that comes off the motor has to sit flush with the longer side of the toothbrush. Cut a little bit off the biro tube to act as a sleeve on the motor's shaft. Push the staple into the sleeve and there's the heart of the machine, like a pen with a paperweight at the top. Then tape the Artline pen, without all its insides, to the long part of the toothbrush, so that the shaft from the motor and the Artline tube (which is now the needle-shaft) are exactly in line. Sharpen the guitar string on fine sandpaper and cut it the length of a needle. Blow all the ink out of the biro. Roll up toilet paper really tight and thin to twist through the biro tube, so you can clean the ink out. Melt the guitar string to the end, put it in the Artline so the needle sticks out past the tip, and at the other end push the staple through the needle shaft so when the motor spins the ink tube goes up and down.

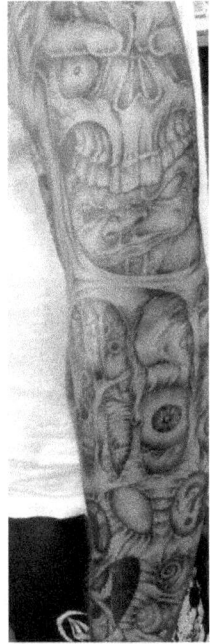

▲ *Boras again on the other arm, more of my freehand work. Many hours of pain for him, just as many of strain for me.*

We had alcohol swabs and lighters to sterilise the needle. Never use the same needle twice so every tattoo he did he had to find a new Artline and needle-tube. After a while we were both tattooing frantically and we cleaned the prisons out of them. It became a rule you had to buy your own. I didn't like the look of the soot ink so I worked another angle. To get some black gold it's not what you know, it's who you know, and you know, I got the special Artline pens from the cleaner. 2200 they were called, and the best blackest ink on the prison market. I could get boxes of them for a packet of White Ox smokes

▲ Thigh tattoo
The skulls on my leg were the first
actual decent tattoo I eva done.

whenever I ran out.

But with tattooing came dramas. Jealous pricks give you up cold because you say you won't tattoo them, or they call you a dog to try to put you on show. I done alright, though. I was only ever called a dog to my face twice in adult prison. The first time I was standing in the cell block talking to another SK member about the tattoo he wanted. This try-hard dickhead from our juvie days walked up and said, "When you doing mine, bud?"

I looked at him and said, "I got too much on. Go see brother-boy upstairs," and went back to talking. It was lock up and we were about to go in our cells and that stupid prick, Jarad Davies, yells out, "Yah, white dog cunt, you'll get yours!"

I looked at my mate and said, "Was that at me, man?" Who was he calling a white dog cunt? For a start he was whiter than me and he was the known dog of the gaol, working for the screws, giving info on the pot-smokers. I seen red instantly, but it was too late do anything. He was locked in his cell and I was about to be locked in mine.

Everyone was calling out to me, "You gonna cop that are you, bro?" I wasn't copping shit. I was waiting, passing time in my cell, angry as fuck, practising what I was going to do to the fucker in the morning. I was going to smash him in front of his boys. I didn't give a fuck, charge or no charge. I had too much to lose out of all this. I was in with the big names of the prison system in Western Australia, their protégé. I would have been a disgrace to my whole crew and my brothers in other crews.

He had a few friends in the gaol that were a bit blind at first, but they learnt the hard way. The next day came and everyone knew it was going to be on. At least from my end, any way. The doors were unlocked at seven. I was waiting, ready. As soon as they called, righto, I was out of my cell. He was walking down from the top landing. I was walking up from the bottom. My heart was racing. I heard a voice behind me yell, "Whoooa!"

I said, "Dog cunt!" and smashed my right hook into his face.

He staggered and I followed with my left. As he fell forward I gave him an uppercut, punching him that many times he was spitting tooth-chips. My hands were busted. I grabbed him by the back of his head and ran at the screws' box, smashing his face into it. The screws shit themselves. The security screen flew up, smashing the bloke's face again. He spun around to punch me and slipped in his own blood, falling back. I went to stomp on his face with my foot. I jumped in the air, going to crush his face, but big Brett Maverick, my trainer for years after, slung me off like a rag doll and said, "He's not worth it, brother."

I was like a dead-set wild animal, frothing at the mouth. The weak prick started crying, saying, "You're fucked. You're fucked." He was gargling on his own blood. He called me a dog again. Brett let me go and I booted him fair in his foul mouth. Then I seen stars because the prison officers skittled me across the room. I just smashed their boy and they weren't happy about it.

That was my first fight in the adult system. One of many.

After I came back around, I found I was being carried down the back by three officers that were not happy with me or my attitude. As far as they could see I was a trouble-maker. That was my first time in the adult prison punishment system. They tried to say I assaulted an officer when they tackled me. I didn't touch any officer at all. They raided my cell and found all my tattoo gear that I'd collected. I was charged with that as well. You get charged for self-harm, assault, if you are caught tattooing or masturbating. And no, I wasn't ever charged with that. I had good ears. They then told me the superintendent would be coming to talk to me later, and I would be going up in front of the visiting justice, which we call VJs in the kangaroo court in prison. The only thing about that court is there is no defence. You are guilty even if you aren't guilty. It's just a room inside the prison set out to look like a courtroom. Everything is the same as a

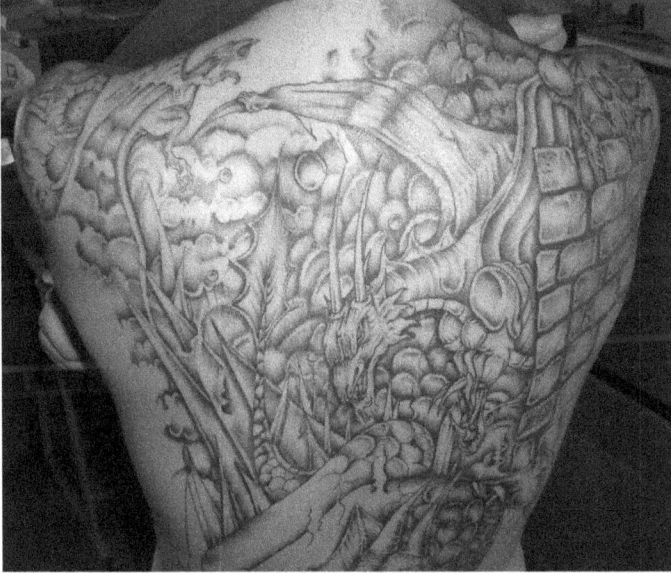

▲ The Back Tattoo

*That is another free hand tattoo I done on a friend Darren. I designed
it myself except the bottom dragon that was a picture from a tattoo
book, but I changed it around a little bit to be one of a kind. It was all
done in Swan Hill 2006.*

courtroom. Put your hand on the Bible and all that sort
of stuff. But really the prosecutors should have to do the
same thing. I was sentenced to seven days down the back
for my naughty behaviour, seven days of close supervision and loss-of-privileges for three months.

These cells were at the other end of the prison. They
didn't look like no other cells I had seen. There was nothing in them at all except the toilet and toilet roll and the
bed frame. I was strip-searched the same way I was on
entry to the prison, the same way you were for every visit,
if you were able to get visits. I lost all privileges for the

175

fight—that's what they call LOP. I wasn't allowed phone calls, visits or any rec time for three months. Not that I got visits anyway, and I had no one worth ringing. I didn't have a TV that I owned.

Two of the brothers that were in single cells with TVs moved into a double cell and I got a nice clean, fresh single cell. It would take me one day and I'd be into the run of things. I didn't have to leave my unit. My tattoo skills got me whatever I wanted. I started tattooing myself because the physical pain was a drug to take away the mental pain. I sat up for twelve hours tattooing my leg one night. I had a new machine and all the bits and pieces I needed. I was in a single cell on my own. I got locked up at seven o'clock that night and by unlock the next morning I had done the top of my right leg: a big skull with a tribal image behind it. When we were released from our cells I went and showed my mate Greg, who had given me the tattoo machine, and he freaked. He didn't believe I had done it myself. And from that moment on I was set. I still had to fight my own battles, I just had a lot more ways of doing things. About three weeks later I had pretty much covered half of my body. I switch off to the pain. It's still there, but I can block it out. If anything, it's a relaxing thing. I always feel tired after tattooing myself or anyone else. I have had plenty of people freak out on me when they have seen me tattooing myself. They always say, "Doesn't that hurt?" Of course it hurts. But it's nothing compared to what I have felt through my life. It helps me remember I am alive. The only thing I hate about tattooing myself all them years ago is I've got shit all over me. The work I am capable of now is a thousand times better. Nowadays I sometimes tattoo a couple of close family members and friends, but that's it. Purely for the love of art. I'll let my photos tell the story for me.

Everyone in prison wants a tattoo, and if you're known for having the clean goods you got what you wanted. My time was made a lot easier because of the skills I had. Sure, it caused problems, because I had prison charges, but that was the price I was willing to pay to get through with no dramas. I tattooed the biggest, baddest brothers in the Western Australian prison system, and there is no room for mistakes when you're tattooing convicted murderers. And I don't mean the bloke that goes out and kills a woman that can't defend herself. I mean blokes that cut people up with axes and put them in garbage bags, or blow their heads clean off with shotguns. I heard some mad stories on the job. A lot of the time, if I was doing freehand work, I'd interpret my view of the person into their tattoo. I mainly did freehand work because I didn't like copying pictures. I got a head full of my own. And I admit I had a couple unhappy customers. But who's to say that wasn't deliberate? Like they say, keep your friends close and your enemies closer.

I had a great enemy in the system: Big Bad Button. I got my own back when I tattooed a penis with a shotgun in his hands and wrote *Slong Hopper* underneath, when he thought he was getting a clown holding the gun. It was supposed to be a gang tattoo, supposed to say *SK Killers*. But the dude never got in the gang. I won't say anymore, because I don't want to incriminate myself. He loved my work.

I did tattoos for access to shives, shanks, knives, whatever you want to call them. I had knuckle-dusters you couldn't even buy on the outside. But it all got found, so relax. This sort of shit was all through the prison. It wasn't mine but I knew where it all was, and I'm not giving nothing up. This was a long time ago and all involved were split up. I learnt from that prison that the first thing you do is arm up to the teeth, have stashes everywhere. Each time I went to prison that's what I done. Get to work in metal work for a while or do some ink work on someone who was working in there.

It wasn't long before I was classed a management problem. I started being a smart-arse to the screws once I was comfortable in my environment. Management problem means I couldn't be told what to do. I saw the prison officers for what they were: exactly the same as me, only they wore suits. Tell me what to do? Fuck that. Get stuffed. Catch them on the outside see how they fly. That's how I thought back then, and I meant it.

My worst enemy was myself, because I created problems for myself by being paranoid and living by the killer rule. Some things I should have stayed out of, or just let go, because I wasn't anywhere near as good or as tough as I thought I was. And I could have been killed easily. I met up with one of the hardest men in the Western Australian prison system, Brett Laverick. One violent man, he was a true gentlemen if you were a friend. He was a Christian man most of the time, well, he tried to be. Sometimes though, I think the brother couldn't remember which side of the fence he was on. He liked me because I reminded him of himself when he went to Fremantle, and because I found it in me to still believe in God, even though I was a fuck up. People stayed the fuck away from him, even the hard nuts of the prison. Brett had trained many people to become fighters over the years, and he done it well. No fucking around, the man weighed at least 130 kilos of ripped muscles. Every day for our stretches he'd stand with his back to the wall and leg lifted and touch his toes on the wall behind him. Brett was a serious trainer and I owe him thanks for all the years he trained me. The style he taught had no name. I called it *Smashing*. It was a mixture of everything he had learnt in his lifetime. When he'd been growing up on the streets that was how he survived. He had fights for money at the back of pubs and nightclubs, underground fighting. Everybody in the prison knew who he was, whether they'd had a punch in the head from him or not.

I trained with Brett for most of my prison terms. Brett couldn't live on the outside. He was at home in prison. He only ever got out for a week or two at a time. Then he would be back for completely destroying some pub on a Friday night, or walking into a bunch of police and going mental. His stories still float around the prisons today, I'd say. When the prison officers got a bit worried about him they came with back up and lots of it. He didn't go off too often, but he obviously did a bit back in the Freo days.

What I liked about Brett was that there was one bloke

in the gaol that I hated and who hated me: little Brad. Brad hated the fact that I had talents that made my life a little bit easier than most. He too trained with Brett. It worked like this: if I'd have touched Brad just out of the blue, I would have been dealt with, no matter who was behind me. But in training Brett would make me spar with Brad and that was where I got what I wanted—open season on his face. I admit the first couple of times I was unsure of hitting Brad because of comebacks. I knew I'd kick his arse, but half the prison was his family.

Brett pulled me aside and said, "What the fuck are you doing? You look stupid. Punch the cunt or I'll punch you." And that was enough for me. It was on. I punched the shit out of Brad. He hated it because he couldn't do nothing about it: it was all part of training. Brett punched me around the room plenty of times, so it was my turn to do the same to Brad.

All the gaol in the world don't mean you're a tough prick. Brad was in for murder and back then I thought that was an achievement.

None of the other white boys I'd done time with in the juvie system were training. They either stayed in their cells all day or they walked around the oval. I trained every day. Brett rolled my shins with broomsticks until they were bleeding. Within eight months I could kick like a horse. Brett focussed on elbows and legs more so than the fists. I loved training. I felt incredible and no one fucked with me. No doubt there will be people who say otherwise. But the truth is known, and I still have the same brothers as I did back then. I got tested by the old-school players plenty of times. Brad was my test, even though I punched him out in the training sessions he still had the power to make my life difficult at times. Mostly by playing mental games. Making me think there was a contract on my head in gaol for something that wasn't even anything to do with me. He had other family of his walk up and have a go at me to see if I'd run to the screws. I never did.

Brad's brother Marty was a better fellow to talk with. He had some morals about him. And he didn't seem like a short arse trying to make up for his size by picking blues with the bigger fellas and getting the family to make sure he didn't get beaten.

Brad hated me most of all because his family member Greg Quartermane was one of my best mates. He took me under his wing when he learnt I was an artist. In Greg's eyes I was just as important as Brad, probably even more. I read Greg's letters to him, because he couldn't read, and in return I got an ear in on all the prison action. And whatever I wanted for my tattooing. I was a big shot at times, and tested out what I was capable of. Let's just put it this way: ink is like cash, and good ink is power. I was the best at it in my time, doing a professional standard tattoo with a bodgy gun. I tattooed bosses of motorcycle clubs, prison gang bosses, Willi Smith, Mick Dershaw. I tattooed a clown on the top of Terry Collier's head. I tattooed notorious armed robber Leon Sutcliffe. I tattooed a Maori brother named Kiwi through a cell window. That was a tribal design on his arse. We got the job done because he was getting changed to another prison. I spent a lot of time in Choky, which means punishment, otherwise known as down the back, for tattooing. And for my attitude problem towards the screws.

There were at least seven officers per unit. They done weekly turnarounds with another crew of seven, and each one of them was warned to watch me, because I had fuck-all tattoos when I entered prison and now I was pretty much covered. I had to learn somewhere.

I had problems with people who didn't want to pay for tattoos. The cheap pricks liked it when I was down the back because they could all relax and not have to look over their shoulders. Like they say: out of sight, out of mind.

But some of my brothers took care of shit for me. I always had smokes when I got out. I didn't really care, because my whole life I was the outcast. I was never meant to be the man that I was. I got trapped in the I-couldn't-give-a-fuck lifestyle. I was an SK gangster as far as I was concerned. I didn't want to live through all the shit I have lived, but I was there amongst it.

Ninety percent of our crew were Noongars, but there were a few white boys. I'll be honest, I thought I was Noongar myself. I wasn't scared to punch on with them like most of the white boys were, and I think that's what got me respect from the brothers. Hanging out with them taught me how to fight. In my younger years I punched on with anyone if I had to, so I wasn't looking for protection, and to be honest no one protects a white boy in prison. That's entertainment for the rest of the boys. If you're getting mobbed, a couple of crew will jump in, but apart from that you're on your own. On the gang front I got respect from my brothers that believed in it, but I still call them sheep.

I don't know how motorcycle clubs work, or any other organisations, but I'd say they're the same: each is for their own. I had a lot of old school club members in prison that told me to avoid the shit if I could, so I did. Bike clubs fascinated me because I love Harleys and partying (well, that's something we all like to do) but I never fit in anywhere I had to answer to someone. I won't talk about things I don't really know anything about, but I will say this: everyone's a hard cunt in a crew, but when you're on your own, you're on your own. Every bird leaves the nest at some stage. It's like this; there is good and bad in everything. I've met some true gentlemen in the biggest organisations in Australia and that's what they are: family men that love their kids like you and I love our kids. But then you get the young up-and-comings that are pure fuckwits. I say that because I was one. Not all the potential crew are fuckwits, but most are. They have something to prove, keen to impress, and want to climb the ladder of status. They also get dealt with from the older crew, too, if they fuck up. It's just like a family, well, like my experience with families.

The police force works the same way. I met a few coppers that were just doing their job. I didn't go have a beer with them or anything like that, they just didn't give me the shits like every other officer. The police force is just another gang, only difference is they have a badge that says *Trust Us.* They use excessive violence when it's not needed. They cause just as many problems as half the gangs in the world. How do you spell organised crime? C-O-P-S. I should have been a copper. I wasn't real good at breaking the law illegally. I should have tried breaking it legally. It's all about strength in numbers, same way we worked in prison. The politicians are the same, they are just the high-roller gang. They live it up on taxpayers' money. Liberals are one gang, Labor is the other. Tell me I'm wrong. There's just as much sly dirty work going on in those places. If the public knew everything the parties would be fucked, too. They're a gang. They bullshit as a united team to benefit themselves. That's what a gang is. Fighting for power, whether it's in a suburb or for a country, you're a gang. Oh, sorry, let's say it properly: you're a party. It should be Liberal gangsters and Labor pranksters. Just the same as most crews, if one gets caught then they all start rolling. And the true staunch ones get left in the wind. That's the way I see it.

Another gang thing in prison is the tattoo. All gangsters want to show their crew-piece.

That was where I came in.

I pretty well breezed through the first time, which made it easy for me to return. I wasn't scared of the place no more. All the brothers I met in there were like my real family, even more so than the boys' homes. Being surrounded mostly by men made me have to mature a little quicker. Today I laugh at the people I met. Some of them I met around the neighbourhood. To the ones that have been to gaol and stand around saying, "I ran that place", "It was my house", or "I was the biggest man in the prison", fuck off! You're full of shit. Only thing you ran was your mouth and you were the biggest bloke around your arsehole. You and I both know there are brothers in there that, if they heard you saying that, you'd be fucked so hard you would start growing tits. That's the truth. Try making every single person in prison fear you. You won't walk out.

• • •

Ray Ray: biggest, craziest Aboriginal brother I ever met. Ray Ray was nuts. If he hit you, you stayed hit. I seen him lift bloke's feet off the ground with one punch. His knuckles were like golf balls. His head told stories of wars. He had scars from beer bottles and whatever else had been across his head. Dreadlocks from hell, all different shapes and sizes. Solid as a brick shithouse. All he knew was fight, and I tell you this: that brother, despite what I say about running a prison, he ran the fucken gaol in the way of violence.

We were cellmates for six months in Casa prison. When I first got there to the main units in 1999, about my third time in the adult system, he and Kingsta and Hawkins were my best cellmates. We had parties. It wasn't gaol. Anyway, Ray Ray was a mad guitar player, slide guitar or whatever. It was mad. He'd play for hours at night while I drew my pictures or tattooed him. Both of us were smashed all the time from the tiniest bit of pot. Anyway,

◄ Acacia Prison
*Me and Aaron one of my
5/8s china plates just
finishing training in the
gym. I was about 25 years
old and had already spent
approx. 8 years behind
bars on and off.*

this one night I don't know what the fuck came over my crazy fucken brother, but he lost it. I think the footy was on and the gaol was going mad. You could hear cell doors getting kicked from the other cellblocks, blokes screaming all sorts of shit.

"Go the Blues!!"

"Get fucked, dogs!!"

All sorts of charming things.

Ray Ray liked footy, too, but he obviously didn't want to hear about it that night. He jumped up from his seat, lifted the sliding window and yelled, "Listen here you fucken dogs, shut your cunts up!" There was still noise, so he just started screaming and kept on screaming until everything went quiet. After about two minutes it all when quiet, but Ray Ray yelled, "Any of you cunts makes another noise I'll catch ya in the morning. Shut your fucken holes, dogs."

Someone yelled out, "Who the fuck's that?"

Stupid prick should have kept his mouth shut. Ray Ray lost it and told the whole prison who he was. I was sitting next to the mad cunt. It was like he didn't even know I was in the cell. The next morning was a Saturday and I slept in until eight o'clock. Before I had even got out of bed Ray Ray had gone and found Lindsey Butts and smashed his big head in, all around the front of the unit. He came back into our cell and said, "Get up, bruz. Get up. Screw's gonna put me away. Bring us smokes, hey?"

I told him no worries and asked what the fuck happened.

He said, "Look out the front there," so I pulled the curtain aside and fuck! There were three blokes out the front of the unit laying on their arses. One was fucked. A big slob in the middle of the footpath: that was Butts. Yogie was lying back, holding his head like it had been split and he was scared it was going to fall open. He was yelling for help. There were screws standing around the other bloke. I couldn't see him. From what I did see, my mate standing next to me was fucked.

We both heard the keys coming running down the stairs. It was the screws. Not one or two, but eight or nine. It was on, and that was the last I saw of my mate for about six months. I took him smokes all the time until he got out. Packet of White Ox every week. He was a true brother, that bloke, and always will be. He made a clear path through the system for me. I ain't scared to admit it, either: he looked after me and had my back, even from down the back in choky. I could look after myself, but I was no hero, and being a brother team with him showed everybody I didn't give a fuck because he didn't hang around with fuckheads and he didn't fight no other prick's battles. He just stood staunch for those who stood staunch for him.

•   •   •

It was always fun to watch the look on the so-called hard, wannabe gangsters' faces when they were on their own. In our world they were that hard they signed themselves up for protection. One day there in mainstream, the next they're gone. You see the officers walk them off with their head down, or they act all hard and shit, yelling out threats. Should have thought about that before they went crying to the screws. If the screws didn't get to their cells and take their belongings or lock the cell quick, the cell's got robbed, stripped like a stolen car in a back alleyway. If you've got no form, stay out of the wannabe shit. You're not a gangster's arsehole. I got form, but I'll admit it: I'm not a gangster. I tried but I couldn't do it. I'm too stubborn, thought my shit didn't stink. It was alright as a kid and in prison, but on the outside—fuck!—there's more to it than just a bunch of brothers getting stoned, tattooing, listening to music, having a fight every now and then. A number of so-called hard men are only so by their own accord and to the run-of-the-mill citizen. How do I know that? Because I called the bluff on heaps of them, most of them are well-known because of rumours—half of which are blown way out of proportion. In all honesty you can be a four-foot fuck-all and have a bad day, catch someone off guard and there you have it: you have the hard prick reputation.

The way I done it was I just played fucken mental. I talked to myself, walked up and down the wing. I was crazy. I made it my point to be crazier than all the other nutters in the place. But that too backfired on me. The prison had to dose me up on medications. I became a walking zombie, doing the large shuffle: rocking from side to side. It was cool. It was all remission to me. I slept heaps of the time. I'd get all worked up, though, and that played against me. I punched into people that didn't deserve it. I was just off my head, looking for someone to take my shit out on.

One time I thought this dude in the cell across from me was doing voodoo on me. He was a freaky looking fella named Jason Spears. Why did I think he was doing voodoo? I don't really know, but he worried me. He was into freaky shit. He had pictures of babies being sacrificed that he had drawn, and some bizarre shit. He even glued real hair on the head of the baby. He was eyeballing me during the muster parade. I couldn't help myself. Still fucked up on the medication, I walked straight in his cell. He followed me, asking what I was doing. I spun around and lifted him with one punch. I went to hit him again, but he was lying back out in the corridor. Then I realised what I had done. Muster wasn't even finished yet. The prison officer ran. I heard his keys as he came to the door. I knew I was fucked and walked out like I

▲ Canningvale Prison

Me and Daniel Tyler, my foster brother and best mate through life on the streets. His mother Kerri helped me out a lot through some hard times. I was about 18 years old.

didn't know what happened. All the other brothers pissed themselves laughing, because I was like a little kid that made a boo-boo. I was then taken to the infirmary, where I was put in close supervision: a padded cell. I was in a karate suit made out of canvas. I spent plenty of time in those things but let's not talk about that now.

• • •

I had a prison officer try coming onto an ex-girlfriend of mine when she visited me, asking for her phone number. When I heard about that I went right off. The fact that he would be a smart-arse and say shit like, "Wayne, your missus won't be home today. She's still recovering from this," and grab his balls ultimately didn't help me much, either. I threw a pool ball at the screw's box. It was the wrong thing to do. I didn't handle the situation properly, but that shit feels good for at least five minutes. After that you're usually getting the fuck kicked out of you by three or more officers. Never any less than two, just in case you turn the table. They've been the victims many times. Some of those screws are big motherfuckers and they aren't shy about knocking a brother out cold. If they couldn't deal with you they would start a rumour that you were child molester, or say you were giving info to the screws. It normally would take about a week, but someone would get you. Put a man in prison, take everything from him and you just set yourself up for a fuck up. If you got nothing to lose then who wins? Yes, I know even if you have nothing to lose some people think there is still your spirit. Well, that's all good if your

▲ *Me in Adelaide on my Harley loving the free life. I built that bike up myself. Lots of blood, sweat and tears. It was given to me from a dear old friend who I'll never forget for getting me started in a new state.*

spirit hasn't already been crushed the way seen it, all day long in the hell-holes. I had people who didn't know shit about me punishing me. Other people saw it the same way. Officers do provoke people to hit them. To try to fuel a reaction. It happens all the time. I seen an officer get his jaw snapped by Lindsey Button in 1997. Lindsey was my sworn enemy, but I give the bloke that. He had a punch and a half on him. And that was over a phone call.

I had my fair share of problems with the officers as well. Whenever they took me down the back I'd never walk for them, they always had to carry me like a hand-bag. I admit I was a smart-arse too. When I got comfort-able in the place I'd back mouth the officers or call them dogs whenever they walked past my cell. That's probably why I got a hard time. I couldn't help myself, though. I honestly hated the prison officers. They were arseholes who locked me away at night with their smart-arse smiles. I still don't like prison officers, but I don't hate them either.

I seen heaps of nice mothers visit their sons on the inside over the years. There every week without fail, looking shattered that their child was in a place of such negativity. I felt sorry for some of the mums, because basically their kids were using them. Not all of them, but you can tell. They are mummy's boys that found drugs, got habits and turned to crime, dragging their whole family down with them. Probably the same as what I would have been doing if I stayed at home. Who knows. They get money off their mum on visits to pay for their drug habit in prison, or money put into their phone so they can ring their so-called girlfriend who doesn't even want to talk to them. They sook around the prison like bitches and their mums suffer for them. I hated them pricks, because all I wanted was a mum and they took advantage of theirs. I admit I got money and things off my mum and dad over the years, but not very often. Once in a blue moon, if I was lucky. And never when I was in the prison system. I say make the prick do it hard. Visit, no worries. But don't give a junkie cash for drugs.

If I had a dollar for every time someone in uniform said to me, "At least I have a home to go to," or, "I'm the one going home tonight," or, "Do us all a favour and top yourself," I would be one rich person.

Not all my dealings with the system have been like that. I don't care how hard a man you think you are: when that door closes at seven o'clock and you sit in that cell you think of a place you would much rather be or a life you would much rather like to live. I got around gaol not giving a fuck because I was not letting no one fuck my arse. I'd stick a toothbrush in your neck. But that don't mean that the fear of some bunch of sick fuckers just mobbing you doesn't roll around in the back of your mind. I was a kid when I entered the adult prison system, well I had the maturity level of a kid. That soon gets snapped out of you. A lot of the long term-ers won't put up with your shit. I was lucky. I had a lot of people watch me grow up through the systems. I was family, but I still had my fair share of shit. Plenty of people who were just bored would try to start shit, or some young prick like I was had something to prove. If you became a target you were fucked. That's how people get by in gaol. A good flogging makes for good entertainment.

One of my best mates Daniel Hawkins was stabbed

more than twenty times in the Canningvale kitchen with a boning knife over an egg. Some young fuck thought he could make a statement. You just have to remember when you walk into the jungle you are entering murder TAFE. One big crime lab. You can come in for stealing a blow dryer but when you leave you are a potential killer. The rage that gets forced into you is not the normal everyday bad temper. You explode. When I went off I went right off, and lucky for a lot of people I had a couple of old mates that actually cared enough about me to sit me down. They would tell me the right way to go about things so I wouldn't get in the shit. I was quite capable of murder. At times I used to want to do things differently. I even thought of biting the jugular out just to show how sick I could be. I bit a fella's ear off, not that I had any choice. I'm sorry. I lie. I had a choice: either get this bloke off or die. And I believe I made the right choice. There are no dirty fighting rules where I come from. It's the will to live. It's smash until someone's dead or in hospital, because in prison most of the people you blew with were either just as fucked up as you or they were doing a paid job. All you are worth in gaol is a packet of White Ox or a bit of pot. I know this because I have smoked dope for a long period of time and I was not going to do no sexual favours, but I had no problems with just punching the piss out of some smart arse in front of a whole prison. If you make a promise you stick to it. If you back down you get dealt with.

In gaol a lot of it has to do with your ego. And if you can get away with something then everybody is going

to think the same and things get blown way out of proportion. If you think you're hard out here, go play with
the hard-ball players where they get their jaws broken
in basketball, legs snapped in football, and put in comas
in a friendly game of tennis. If you jump in the phone
queue or you're seen on the phone too much, you are
in with a real good chance at having the phone mouth-
piece smashed over your face. If you get around doing it
hard you are also in with a good chance of a mobbing,
because if you are mobbing around you will bring other
people down around you who probably have more to
be down about than you do. No one in there is going to
give a fuck about your hard life story. In there you are
just a fresh fish and there are plenty of sharks that are
hungry, so when you are big shotting in front of your
mates and you think you are all that, well I hope for
your sake that you are as good as you think. When you
walk around in prison and you get that uneasy feeling
that something is not right, you should really take note.
Chances are that you are being sized up for any number
of things. If you live by the knife you are going to get
served by the knife. Once you are known for putting
holes in people, then people get scared and, like myself,
they hit the problem chest-on. Maybe not chest-on, but
from behind in the showers, in the toilet, in the gym, on
the way to a visit. You can't win. There is always that one
person who will go that little bit further to put a point
across.

Anyone that adopts a life of crime, you may think it's
all good, high-rolling with the cash, fancy motel rooms,

spas, girls, everything you want. Well, be prepared for food that some sick fuck has tampered with, lock in at seven, visits once a week, limited phone calls, and prison officers that are on power-trips. Some days you don't even get let out of your cell. You could be sharing a cell with anyone, from an undercover tamp to a sick serial rapist, or someone who is likely to stab you if you shit after lockdown. You can laugh, but I am telling you, even when you think a life of crime does pay, man, you wait until shit starts falling because when it rains it pours. No one is that good that they never get caught eventually. You get bitten by the hand that feeds you. It's Murphy's Law.

Honestly when you sit in that cell and you know that the next day is going to be a mental and physical war you want nothing more than to go back and change the road you took, whatever the cost. But I am sorry to say at that time, at that moment, you are completely alone with how you are feeling. There is nothing you can do about it. That's where deaths in custody come into the picture, and there are plenty of those. In my honest opinion, some of those deaths have a bit of a helping hand. They did when I was around in the system. Of course, I have no proof so it never happened.

Really what I am saying is this: the prison system is one big evil circle of shit, you regret it in the end.

Once you have a record for armed robbery, assaults, car theft, you are pretty well fucked in the public's eyes. Gaol leaves a scar that you can't see but people can sense. I walked around with my hands behind my back for two years when I got out. I still call everyone bro, even the women. Or I call them Boss. People can tell from the way you speak. People would cross the road when I was walking towards them, or they asked me, "How long have you been away for?"

They don't do it anymore, but it did happen and anyone that has been in prison knows what I am talking about.

Away from home, you come back different: anti-social, still in prison in your own mind. It takes a long time to get your shit together. Not everyone is the same, but once you have been to prison you usually return to see the place. Most young people see gaol as a scary place, but once they go there they might do a little time and get out before they get to see the real unmasked life in prison. When they come back, however, and it's for a real whack of time, they soon realise prison is like a sand dune. It can be in one place one day and the next it could be the complete opposite. Your friends from one day turn on you the next. If someone doesn't like you all they have to do is start a rumour and the wind will do the rest. He said, he said, you said—rumours can get you in a whole lot of shit. You might say you don't trust someone, and by the end of the day it's getting around that you said you want to cut his head off. That shit happens. The people that start the rumours don't give a fuck that it's not true, they just want to see some action. Or see if you can look after yourself. If someone pulls a knife on you in gaol, that's it, you are going to get stabbed. If not on that day, it's coming. Either you arm up or go to protection or get transferred as quickly as possible. Not everyone that is in protection is a dog, just most of them. Just because you're scared doesn't mean you're a dog. Every single person at some stage in their life has been frightened, when they just wanted to hide. Not all of us are the same, but the ones in protection that are scared really need to check their life plan, because prison life don't get any better. Don't throw what you can't catch.

I look back on things now and I get butterflies in my stomach. I am no expert on life but I am an expert on fucking up, and my mind has opened up to so much since I have been straight. A word of advice to anyone in prison being fucked with: don't play their games.

• • •

I came up for parole just after I turned twenty. Getting parole was an experience. It was different to the juvenile centres, where you got probation and things like that. It was all organised for you when you were young. In prison you had to do it yourself. There was a system: if it was your first time on parole you had automatic parole. You pretty much got out on your release day. If you were in for a breach of parole your file went up for review in front of six people called the parole board, and they had the power to knock you back or let you go. Everyone is given a parole officer when they go up for parole. Their job is to go around and make sure everything you say on your parole plan is true.

For parole I had to have an address I could live at that was stable. I used my parents'. I hand it to my mum that she helped me get out on parole once, but I was still fucked up. I had to do urine tests every week for the first six months of my parole. I had two years to do the parole. I had to report to the office regularly. I didn't go live at home. I just went back to what I knew: being a crim. I was an adrenaline junkie now as well, because the feelings I got when I was committing crime as an adult were different to when I was a kid. I was a man now. Throw a hit at me and see what happens. That was the way I saw it. *I'll take your fucken car off you—what are you going to do?* I had a bigger chip on my shoulder than I'd ever had. I thought my shit didn't stink, but I breached my parole within a few weeks for failing to report. I would have been dirty if I did a urine test, so I chose not to show up. I got a bit of a buzz being on the run. At times it made me feel important. It's okay when you have nothing to lose, or when you think you have nothing to lose, but there are other times in life that you will want to settle down and you'll find it not real easy.

When you get told you are something so many times, you start to think that's who you are. All I was ever told or led to believe was that I was an arsehole, a cunt, criminal, anti-social, psycho, demon, piece of shit, and a whole lot more charming things. I was told I was institutionalised so I believed it. When I was free, that was a holiday. I believe when you go to prison, time stops. Your body grows older but your mind stays pretty much the same. I think because you're not living a normal lifestyle you don't really mature in the way of everyday living. That's why I think it is hard for so many people who go to prison for a fairly long period of time to readjust to society. I got out of Riverbank when I was just about eighteen. I still felt fifteen. I got out of Casa when I was twenty, but I still felt about seventeen. When I was released from Canningvale at the age of twenty-six I was eighteen in my mind.

My view on the parole system used to be: it's set up to fail. If someone on the parole board doesn't want you on the streets, they can breach you anytime and keep on doing it for as long as they like. You can't live life as a normal citizen. When I was on parole the pricks trying to run my life in prison still ran it on the outside. Now as a mature man, out of the system for a while, I see that parole works for those who make it work. If you are dead-set about getting your life together, parole won't seem like too much of an issue. I had the same parole from when I was eighteen still hanging over me when I was released at twenty-six. I completed it for the first time when I left Western Australia and moved to Adelaide. That was with thanks to some close friends. I owe everything I have today to those people, just for getting me out of Western Australia when they did. I'll be honest though, I fucked up when I lived with them. I still took drugs, and had too much going on in my life emotionally. I chose a woman over family. Not the woman I'm with now, just some girl I thought I loved. All I really wanted was a companion.

As I grew I ended up seeing some of the people who

played a part in my nightmares. Not all of them, mind you, but to be honest they were the clumsiest fellows you could find. Always hurting themselves. This one time a certain fellow by the name of Jarad, well his head got stuck under the hot-water urn. First thing in the morning, too. He came in the night before off the streets, so I just put it down to drugs. He must have nodded off while making a brew, pulling the lever to on as he fell into the sink. It made a real mess of his head. Like I said, I am a firm believer in Karma.

WHOS GOT THE BEATS II

Kids on their own
Dark time they roam
Heads full of pain
By the time they grown
Every single day
They fall victim to the system
Send em to jail
Getemworkinginthekitchen
Learn one way
One way of life
Only friend they know is
Live by the knife

Years move on tears dried up
All emotions gone
They emptied the cup
paranoid thoughts
Hate for the courts
Dirty old men
Wigs pulling ill rorts
No feelings felt
Useyourchildhoodagainstyou
Its all in the reports
Passed on to the screw
Youre just scum
the lowest of low
Piss in a cup
Down the back you go
Provoked to the edge
Revenge is the pledge
All games lost
From kicking in heads
Nightmare flights
Sleepless nights

They smash your spirit
Then they take your rights
Call me an animal
call me what you like
I snapped the damn leash
Now watch this brother psych

Im not evil but evil dwells
I got pain you see my head just swells
Im just a man trying to get it right
Ive been smashed to pieces
All I knew was fight
Ive been punished
My names been rubbished
I done my best
You will see it when im finished
At times I went and lost control
Turnedongodlthoughthestolemysoul
But all things changed
Like its been pre-arranged
I look in myself
Brother I aint strange
Life offered me a plate full of shit
And I ate its filth bit by bit
Then my mind tricked
I got the raw twitch
Got sick and tired of having my
arse cheeks kicked
Trained myself mentally
Drained all emotion
Mixed pain hate and anger
And this is the potion

Wayne McKay

8

BELONGING

When I was released in 1999 I stayed with a family I met through an old Portuguese man in prison. I called the man my boss, out of respect. When he came to prison, he'd never been in trouble with the law. He was scared. I saw it and so did all the prison stand-overs. When people saw him walk back from the canteen they would all hit him up for smokes. I sat back and watched. As the days went by he started saying "No," and then the question became more a threat: "Give us smokes or else."

I thought to myself, *This fella is going to get hurt.* The chances he had at getting through one more day were not looking good.

The next day I was sitting out on the step having a coffee and the old boy walked out from the wing and was real upset. I looked at him and said, "Oi, come over here old boy. Pull up a step."

He was a bit unsure of me, but I put him at ease by saying, "I been here a long time mate, and I don't have to make any new friends, and I got my own smokes. The reason I said to take a seat is because you look like you're about to die, and I don't want the blame for that shit."

He gave me a smile and sat there with me, spinning out on the fact that I was so comfortable. He asked how long I had left and at that time I said to him, "I ain't getting out. This is my home. And even if I do get out, I'll be back within a couple of weeks. This is my home. I don't fit in out there. In here, I know where I stand. The only thing you're missing in here is a lady. I've got plenty of books if you're strung out." The old boy could not believe what he was hearing.

I asked him what he was in for. He told me he was set up, and I laughed and said, "You too, huh? We're all innocent in here. You'll fit in fine."

He said, "No, I really was set up."

I still did not believe him, even after he told me the whole story. I guess after a while you hear so many stories they all sound the same.

The next day I met him out the front again. But this time when I walked out I saw a big black fella take a swing at him for saying no for a cigarette. Normally I would not get involved, but fuck, this bloke was fifty-six and the fella that hit him would have been twenty-five. So I ran over and king-hit this big prick and dropped him on his arse. He fell down the steps and lay on the ground. I walked down to him and shook him.

I said, "You wanna pick on old fuckers, mate? You go to six block and if you want to go on with it after this cunt, you wanna arm up."

One of my big Noongar brothers, Ray Ray, came over to us and said, "What happened?" So I told him, and before the fella could get up he had the fuck kicked out of him for trying to stand over people from our block. The old boy did not know what to say and took off inside to his cell.

About an hour later I walked into his cell and asked if he was alright. He was that thankful he started promising me that he was going to return the favour, set me up once I got outside. I just said, "Old boy, you don't owe me shit. And stop with that setting me up shit. I've heard it a million times and I still ain't got shit. But I have made sure plenty of fellas have got home safe. That's life. I don't want nothing from you. Just keep yourself out of the shit so I don't have to baby sit."

He had no TV. In fact, his cell was bare. So I said, "Come sit in my cell. I got brews and you can watch the news."

When he walked in my cell he couldn't believe it. He saw how comfortable I was in my cell. Everything was in its place. Posters on the walls and all my paintings I had done. Some of my artwork is pretty painful stuff, and as you could imagine the old boy looked at my art and thought I was some serial killer. I had to tell him that the shit he saw in my pictures were not things I had done. They are actually my interpretations of what has happened to me in my life.

After a few weeks went by the old boy ended up moving in with me. Things ran smoothly for him after that. He did his time easily. Throughout, he kept making promises, that for helping him he would help me get out. Me being me, I just said, "Yeah, no worries." I didn't expect anything from him at all, and then when he got out he was actually sad to say goodbye. As far as he was concerned I was his new son. I did not pick up on it because I had heard it all before.

A week went by and I was called up for a money receipt. I did not even get visits or phone-calls, so I was a bit shocked to find a thousand dollars in my account. Luckily the good old system works: my money was frozen until I was released. But that was cool, I did not need no money anyway. I already had all I needed.

The next day I received a letter from the parole board saying they had received a parole address and a plan for work. I tripped right out. I was not even worried about parole. I did not even think I was in with a chance, that's why I hadn't put my parole plan in.

The next mail-day I got another letter, which said, I told you I was innocent. The old boy had spent a quarter of a million dollars fighting to prove his innocence— and he won. And he had plans for me. I got a visit from his wife the following week. I've never been so shy in all my life. I had not had a visit for twelve months, and if I had it was with a psych or a lawyer. This was a lot different. I walked out and this little lady about five foot and with a European look was sitting there smiling. Her face had the look of a lady who had worked very hard all her life, but her eyes were a gentle mother's eyes. I introduced myself and asked if she would like a coffee. She had white with one sugar. After I had returned with the cups of coffee, we sat and talked about the old boy and how he was doing. She kept on thanking me for helping him come home safely, and I honestly did not see what the big deal was. To me it was just another day in the jungle. She explained to me that they had had been talking about me, proposing that I go and live on their little farm just out of Perth. I was spinning right out on all this stuff that was happening for me.

After the visit things just seemed to keep going my way. I was released on parole a short time after—and that's when I fell into the trap. I thought that these people I had met really cared about me.

I used to want to fit in that bad, I would do anything just to be accepted into a crew, gang or family. I would bash the biggest fucker I could find just so I could fit in. I'd do tasks no one else would do, then I would wait for a bit of praise. I was the perfect hunting dog. I did not want much. I had no one, loved violence, and was loyal as fuck. I got that crazy with anger I would attack myself and then just sit in the corner rocking. The more I was treated like a psycho the more I acted it out. I was used as a weapon of torture, sicked onto anyone who disrespected my adopted prison family.

And then I was brought back to the farm.

I had my own house, a two-storey shed. I worked all day landscaping around the farm. Big fancy cars would pull up all day. No one was allowed to talk to me because my boss trusted no one, only me. He could not understand me. He always asked me what I wanted and all I could ever come up with was a motorbike, so he got me a four-wheeler. That used to piss him off. He would hire hookers, pay for them to drive a hundred kilometres to the farm, and all I would do was sit and talk to them. His wife used to tell him, "Wayne's a nice boy. He needs a nice girl."

I seen millions of dollars go over his table and I always kept it safe. No one moved a finger the wrong way when I was in the room. My boss was no Mafia or gangster organisation. In fact, he was a retired cray-fisherman from Portugal that lots of people ripped off over the years. And I was the craziest person the old boy had ever met, so he set me up with all the scariest looking tools he had lying around. People owed him money because he had to sell his crayfish boats whilst in prison. I had a collection of special tools hanging around my room for special occasions. My favourite was the drill. As soon as I pulled the drill out, cheque-books or briefcases would appear. No one got the police involved because of the shonky shit they must have been up to. I was that nice I'd even ask you what size drill-bit would you like? Push it through your foot? Your knee?

It was the only thing I ever got any praise for, so I done well at it. I acted all crazy and like I was capable of anything and my boss would be telling me to calm down. I always got our money, and thankfully I never had to use the drill because that was not who I was. But I very well could have been. I scared a lot of people very easily because of my permanent frown, and I honestly was a person that wanted so badly to fit in. The people I lived with knew that. I know most people would think I was cold, well that was true, but the way I saw it then was: *this is the only chance I am ever going to have at making it in the real world.* I excelled. I trained every day. I was not very big, but I was fast and hard. I loved conquering whatever task was in front of me. I thought I was a somebody. I thought they cared about me. Well, they did care, but still I was being used as a guard dog to protect the old boy. My boss didn't believe in banks, so he was easily ripped off. Now that I think about it, he probably had some enemies as well from the court case he won.

I thought it was all great at the time. I felt like I always wanted to feel like I was a somebody. Everything I ever wanted was at my fingertips: good food, nice warm bed, no bars on the windows. I loved my life. But it wasn't long before I was introduced to the drugs again. Good money bought the good gear. It was my idea, I suppose. I ended up using the gear instead of selling it. I left the farm because I couldn't be trusted around all the money. I left there with a drug habit. I ended up back in prison again. And the old boy died of Ross-River fever, and that was the end of that for me. I couldn't go back. Before he died he used to tell me he was going to buy me a house, help me get my licence, all I had to do was work. It never turned out.

Once again I didn't finish my parole. A desperate lonely person will do anything to fit in. Put a gun in my hands and I'd shoot, no problems at all. It's not until later when you're doing the time for the crime that you realise, *Shit, man, where are my mates now? I thought they were family. Doesn't family stick together?* Then it hits you: family, what did a family ever mean to you? Let your guard down for a minute and you are fucked. Back to being a single soldier. I got real pissed off when the old boy died. Because as fucked as I thought the whole situation was, when I was out I loved the old prick. He was going to help me get out again, give me another chance. I thought it was life's way of saying, *Suffer.* I was left with nothing except my clothes and some tools that would soon get me in trouble. I went back to what I knew best: drugs and crime.

I look back now and think to myself, *How far have I come in my life?* I think maybe that everything I ever went through was not for me, but it was for all the street kids and battlers to learn from. I don't know how but I hope my book, in some way, will help them get through times when they just feel like lashing out at anyone for some payback. Or going to do something stupid to fit in somewhere. Because as bad as life may get, as hard as the road may seem, there is a light at the end of the tunnel. Even if there's not one for miles, it's there. *It can't rain all the time.* I heard that in a movie, and it works for me.

It is not easy if you are all you have and there's no one else to worry about. It's hard to adopt a lifestyle where you have to use emotions to communicate. I still have big problems with feeling for people when someone close to them dies. I feel sorry for them, but to me death is death. On the same token, I only just had someone die that was close to me. I think many years of not caring about life in general fucked my emotions a bit, but now I'm coming back to reality. My wife's stepfather just passed away and I miss the man's face.

• • •

My partner sometimes tells me I am not very affectionate. I think a cuddle now and then is showing love, but there are so many different things involved in loving and I am still learning them. Love is not someone who asks you to shoot. They just don't want to do the gaol themselves, and they don't want the blood on their hands. There is probably only one man I can think of that ever gave me a chance and did not ask for nothing in return, but everyone else would have thought this fellow would want something. My boss at the time was a fair man, despite what society may say about a biker. He owned a tattoo shop in Adelaide (I won't say the name). I wasn't involved in anything to do with clubs, I just had a steady job, one that I could use to start to go places. Before I met my boss I had only ever used home-made tattoo machines. He opened my eyes to a whole new world of art tattooing, alongside a true professional. the sky was my limit.

My boss was more like a brother-figure to me. At the time I was going through hell re-adapting to society. He helped where he could, but I was not ready to be helped. I was too immature in the ways of everyday life. I'd only been out of prison a short time, I had the police watching me, thinking I was involved in some crime syndicate. Before I started working it was all bullshit. I was terrorising people on my own accord, no gang life, no nothing. No one could say I used anyone's name to do my dirty work because I was doing what I was doing as a single soldier. Most of my life, the only times I was involved with gangs was as a juvenile and in the adult system. I worked on my own on the outside because I didn't fit in with anyone. And I didn't trust anyone anyway: DTA.

I ended up messing up because I was a loose cannon on drugs. I started avoiding my work, and went on the run thinking I was a man when really I was a kid in a man's body. I had a job that in twelve months I could have been the best tattooist in Australia, but too much was going on in my life and I thought, *What the fuck? This is too much. Yesterday I had nothing. Today I have a job, my own keys to the shop, and I'm trusted with the alarm.* Too much of a system overload.

▲ *Michele and me just after moving to Geelong. Ready to start a new life. We're sitting down on the waterfront happy as can be.*

I did not rip my boss off at all, that is one thing. I was just unreliable when I had work to finish. That's how I fucked up again. That is probably my biggest regret, because that fellow is someone I will always admire. But I think I pretty much pissed him right off. The one person you think won't give you a chance actually does and you fuck it up. It leaves a scar.

I was a dickhead, leaving the job.

I went the way I did because it was the way I always went. I ran from my problems. After that fuck-up I really did not care about my life. I gave up on myself and went back to the drugs. But it wasn't for long. I met a lady by the name of Michele, who changed my life.

When I first started seeing Michele I was finding it hard to be accepted into society. I did whatever I could to put a smile on someone's face. I have not been an arsehole all my life, it's just that the people I've ever done anything for are battlers, single mothers whose ex's give their kids Playstations and then sell them again for drugs. I would buy bikes, pet puppies, fix old-timer's cars on the side of the road, stop kids from fighting in the park—anything I could do that was endearing. I don't want nothing for anything I ever done, I just want them to have as good a life as they can get in the world they live in. Today I'll help anybody I think needs help, if I possibly can. Anybody that knows me for who I really am knows that I have a giving heart. I'm not greedy or selfish. I've witnessed that my whole life and I didn't like it. I like giving gifts to people when they least expect it. I have had new tyres put on a car for a fellow who had no cash and was a single dad. I do what I can for no other reason but because I want to. I've put myself out for people plenty of times, whether they remember or not.

I feel better about myself when I do good things.

And I want people to eat their words, remembering what they said about me.

I have a bigger heart than most and my heart aims for the right people: the people who are condemned to a life of suffering through no choice of their own. Or somehow they were cast out. For whatever reason it may have been:gay, lesbian, religious, financial, whatever it is. I have done my time in the pain-cooker. All I want to do is tell my side of the story. And hope somebody can get a clear view of what I am trying to say. If it can help anybody from going down the same road, well, I will have done something positive and that's all I want.

If you get thrown off, it's because you are actually watching a man change. I still learn every day and I still get angry with things that happen in my life. But I look for the positive things around me to pull me through, instead of just giving into the negative way I used to. I am far from perfect. I don't want to be. But I'd rather be a positive influence than a negative one.

▲ *Just after I met Michele our first xmas together as a family.*
A changing point in my life. Jayden & Ryley with plenty of presents to
open.

LITTLE DIAMONDS

Littlediamondandmytwostaunchleopards
True-bornleadersdontfollownoShepherds
You got to reach for the skies
And dont spill Em no lies
It aint no myth coz every man cries
Iveseenyouallshinepulledyouallintoline
The life that you live it wont be mine
Dont ever forget those who are real
Only a few care how you feel
Dont sit at a table and play cold deal
Listen to your dad papa raw deal
I watch you laugh and Ive seen you cry
Im doing what I can and that aint no lie

Look at you now
You my favorite songs
Music to my ears cant do me no wrongs
You seen a lot in your little time
Dads got a past I will tell you some time
Dont listen dont listen
To everything you hear
Dont listen dont listen
Theres truth in a tear
Im here for you and all that I do I do for you
Walking big shoe aint done till its through
No more living in the back of the queue

One way or another Ill get to the top
Nomoreputtingfoodbackwhenweshop
No more threats to turn off the power
No more orders coz we are in power

No more waiting for a rort
No more summons for Dad to court

No more second hand living
Had hand me downs
We can start giving

I want you to know no matter what
No matter where
I love you kids
And I will always care
Sometimes you seen me real mad
You seen me hit a man
That was acting out bad
Them things that I have done I am trying
To change
Ivefeelingsnowseeofawholedifferentrange
Megoforwalksandtakecareofmylittleones
One cute daughter and two staunch sons
NobodynowherecouldchangethewaythatI
love and I care
AndiftheywouldtryIwarnthemdontdare
You little ones have my heart
Top of the chart the world is the board and I
am the dart

Know this and know that
Dadclimbedoutfromthebottomofthepack
Know that and know this
Each word that I write is sealed with a kiss
Dad loves you no matter where he is
Everything I do Im doing for you kids
Ive been a bad man
But thats not who I am one day you will see
Your dad had a plan

Wayne McKay

MY ART AND PASSION FOR STREET BEATS

I have been drawing for as long as I can remember. I learnt from watching my granny draw when I was about five years old. She always set me up with paper and crayons when she was painting or sketching. That was our bonding time. My granny was one of the most brilliant realist artists. She could draw or paint anything she saw to perfection. She spent months on one piece. There were always at least three or four artworks going at one time, much the same way I paint now. I went through life with an interest in artwork because of my granny. And I excelled.

I found my style in Casurina Prison with help from the best artists I have ever met in my life, or seen works by: Dennis Nozworthy and Shane Finn, two masters in their own right. My strongest influence was Dennis. The

My painful portraits
▲ *Michele, my partner, we both had a laugh whilst taking photos to do these pictures.*
▼ *Me 5150 criminally insane. I've done a few more for other people, they like to see themselves messed up.*

minute I saw his style of work I fell in love with the way he could portray pain. That was what I was trying to say in mine. His life was very different to mine and I wouldn't think of trying to compare them. He spent a lot longer than me in the prison system, being one of the last men sentenced to hang in the Fremantle prison before they abolished the death sentence. His artwork told his story well. He was like a father figure to me throughout my times in Casurina.

I met him in the art class. I used to sit and have cups of tea with him listening to his gaol stories. He was a fucken legend, strong as an ox, and he took no shit from anybody. He and Shane were both very respected men amongst the inmates. Anytime I needed help or art materials they were both ready to assist me. Shane made me work hard before he'd help me out, because too many blow-ins came to the art room and just fucked around. But when I started drawing they soon saw how serious I was.

Nozworthy's work influenced my own. I tried to use the same shading technique and his distortion of shapes is sometimes visible in my own work, but at the same time I have my own style and try not to use anything he would be using. I'd like to say thank you to them both for all they have done for me. I told them I wouldn't forget.

They both helped me build up the courage to enter my work in the art exhibition held in the closed-down Fremantle Prison. In that exhibition I sold a few pieces. I owe a big thanks to the art coordinator, Zoy Grizzel. She helped me when I was inside and when I was at TAFE on the outside. She gave me paints and all the materials I needed to find my passion, especially for air brushing. Zoy worked hard to push me to try different styles and helped me earn my Certificate in Art and Design.

This is the first certificate I can remember getting since I received one at school, when I was about 9 years old. It hangs above my computer right now as I write this book.

My name was mentioned in the Art Chronicle magazine, after the art exhibition in Fremantle in June 2001. Once I was out of prison I only done art in little doses, until I met my partner Michele. I think I could only really get into it when I was completely comfortable. And I'm comfortable now.

My art will shock. It will leave people thinking, just as my rhymes will. But I just want to say this: what you see and what you hear are just forms of art. I'd rather paint

Me and my two tuff sons visiting me at Ivanhoe Prison Farm. I went back in for 3 months. It was the hardest jail I ever done due to having family on the outside to worry about.

and draw it, sing it or rhyme it, than go out and commit it. My art is my release. It is my channel for whatever emotion I feel. If I don't want to confide I express it in a form that I find peace and strength in. It's a meditation. It's my drug. My escape from the world we live in when I need to get away.

• • •

I never had any musical lessons, except for hearing my granny play when I was a kid. I never sung on a mic except once in karaoke. All through my times in gaol I wrote short poems. I hated the system and voiced my opinion in my rhymes. I always sung along to 2Pac, Snoop Dogg and Doctor Dre. All the gangster beats. It gave me a drive when I heard them, got my heart pumping. I never thought I'd rap on a microphone though.

Rap was just something I listened to, until I got out

of prison for the last time. Then I got mad. I got pissed because I nearly missed the birth of my daughter. I was going straight, living in a little town called Swan Hill.

I had written about 60 rhymes while I was in prison. I said all kinds of nasty shit to deal with the emotions I was feeling inside, not being with my family, my pregnant lady, my two boys. I was in a foreign state. I didn't even know where I was on the Australian map—Ivanhoe Prison Farm, somewhere in the middle of the desert. That was enough to make me say, *Fuck this. I've had enough of this shit, of being pushed around.* I got out and a friend of mine, Greg, had a PA set up for his guitars. We got to messing around one day and he told me to have a go on the mic. The smart-arse turned it right up when I started talking. It nearly blew my eardrums out and I sounded like a dickhead. I threw it at him and said, "You fucken do it. I'll write the words, you sing 'em."

But he wouldn't, so my family got tormented for eighteen months as I began to teach myself at home.

I basically swapped talents with Greg. He was a born tattoo artist, he just didn't know it. He could draw brilliantly. All he needed was someone to give him a push, just as I needed with my music. He went away to his house and drew for twelve months, then I set him up with a tattoo machine. I traded him for his PA system and head-unit and a CD recorder for artwork: I tattooed his forearms freehand, so we both got something we wanted out of it. I collected bits and pieces by tattooing friends. I had guitars, motorbikes, all sorts. I bought a computer programme that made beats, but the thing was

I still didn't know how to use a computer. As it turned out, the one I had was nowhere near advanced enough to do what I wanted to do, so Peter at the music shop took the program and the guitar back and I swapped them for a Zoom drum machine.

That was it: I was on my way. I didn't care what people said. People thought I was dreaming. Some still think I am, but they will see what I have done in the time I have done it. Given enough time I can do whatever I want. Eight months after I started I had my first song played on the local radio station.

It happened like this. A friend, Tamara, who I met when I rode down to the radio station, listened to one of my demos. She told me about a hip hop course for the youth in the town. She organized for me to go sit in and see what they were doing. That was where I met Stuart Holt, my first producer. He invited me to his recording studio at his house, called Shed Recordings. He liked my words and soon put some guitar to them, as well as some beats I made up on the drum machine.

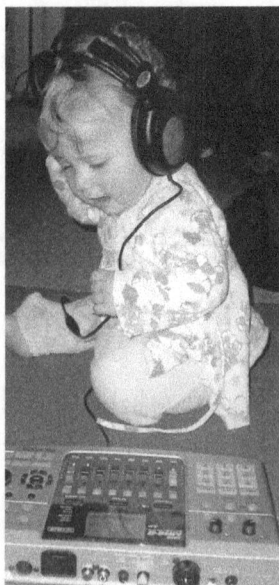

I walked away that day with my first recorded song,

◀ Tahni listening to her Daddy's songs. Something she loves doing. This was when she was about 8 months old and at my first recording studio.

Ashes to Ashes. That was the first song I had played on the radio. All the people who knew me couldn't believe someone who looked like me could say or think the things I was saying in my rhymes. The stories I told were real.

I swapped another guitar to record my second song. It was about my daughter, called *Wake Up Tahni.* That was a song everybody loved and it was played a lot of times. People always stopped me and asked, "Is that you singing, Wayne?" Or, "I heard your song today on the radio." Tamara always supported me and my music, telling me she could see big things in what I was doing. She saw how far I had come. I was an ex-heroin junkie that came to town on methadone. I withdrew from that without no doctor's help. I jogged and sweated it out. The Kent's Pharmacy helped me. I asked if they could withdraw me without me knowing until I was off the methadone completely. I was sent to prison before I was completely off it, for all the dramas I had in the town. I went cold turkey in prison. Not that I had much choice. I was sixty-three kilos on entry. When I was released, three months later, I was ninety-five kilos, the heaviest I had ever weighed.

The day I got out, the whole town saw the change in me and no one could say they didn't. That's how I got to do what I done. I didn't bullshit. I rode around on my bike, went looking for places that could point me in the right direction to help me further my music, such as Tamara.

I met some shonky people through my music who

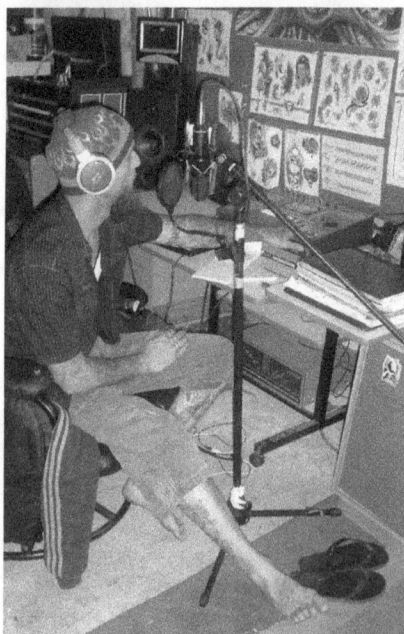

had ill intentions, but I met others too. I know this may sound corny, but this happened. One morning I was lying on my couch, thinking to myself, *How am I going to get a recording studio?* I prayed for the first time in a long time, and this time I didn't ask for nothing. I just said thankyou to God for the wonderful things I had, and thanks for giving me a go. That's all I done. Then I went out the back and was working on a plan. I was going to sell my three-wheeler and buy the studio. That's when there was a knock at the door. Peter from the music shop said, "This is from someone who loves what you've been doing." An anonymous donor gave me music gear; a mini eight-track zoom recording

◄ *Photos of me in my studio at home. Doin' what I love. Recording my songs—my escape from reality.*

studio, exactly what I wanted and needed to move forward. I was stoked. I looked at him and said, "You fucking with me, Peter?" The first thing I actually thought was, *I haven't stolen shit from your shop, man.* But I was cool. It was a friendly visit. I was speechless. Tears came to my eyes and I'm not ashamed to say that either.

From there I went on to record myself and learn a bit about what I wanted to do with my music. I made my own drumbeats and bass tracks just by knowing what I liked to hear. Tamara from the radio station pushed me to go on with what I was doing, always giving me positive drive. Michele, my partner, just spins out on me because I adapted so quickly, and all the young lads around the town loved my music. Seeing what I was capable of blew Michele away. She is my strength. If anything I do sounds shit she tells me straight out, even if I argue the point.

I ended up finding out who donated the studio because he came and saw me and offered to be my manager. All I will say on that for now is, I almost lost my family and everything I worked for because of one ill man. He wasn't a manager at all. He was a con man with lots of money who was using the word of God, and people's kindness and dreams, and then ripping these things out from underneath them. There are some evil people out there who have the best sheep's clothing money can buy. I'll say this to him: convincing yourself you are doing good when you know everything about you is a lie, and then using God's name to do it—you are a dead soul. I hold no grudges because I know you will destroy yourself in the end. You were just a stepping-stone to help me and my family get that little bit stronger for what is yet to come in our life. Thanks. I take what that man did to me and my family and use it as a lesson for everyone I meet. People that come and offer you all your family's dreams, claiming they are doing it for God, be careful and look into it, because God don't give no one permission to bullshit.

My music is all about people like him, *Mr Misery.* I want to give something to the people most likely to grow up to be criminals. Take the other road.

My emotions are in my music. I say some very strong things, but that's how it's seen today. Take what I say anyway you like. What would you rather: a fella who found his way in life and found a love for art, or someone who stresses out with no release and loses it, dragging people down around him? I can't work in the everyday workforce because I don't fit in.

There are too many fuckwits out there. I'm not the smartest man around and people take advantage of that, try to rip me off. So I do what I do best: I create art work and share it with others. I sing about the politicians, the system that screwed me as a kid, I tell people what I was thinking as I was walking.

I don't want people to use my words for bullshit. I was crazy as fuck once upon a time. In my music I am celebrating the fact I got my shit together. I tell the dickheads that haven't lived the gangster lifestyle on the streets, who haven't grown up in the shitholes, to stop talking shit in their trumped up gangster beats. They're all sooks, spreading a bullshit message. Aussie rappers that think they are American, they're sheep. Don't get me wrong; I love American hip-hop. It's where I found my path. But I'm Aussie. I sing about an Aussie lifestyle: mine. It's not about bling bling or any of the Tinsel Town bullshit. It's about putting food on the table and setting up my kids' futures as good as I can. Dig down in the lower income areas and pull out some roses. Like I said before, everybody wants to be loved and everybody wants to be happy. People have the same drive no matter where they're from. It's just not easy being accepted in the big game of survival.

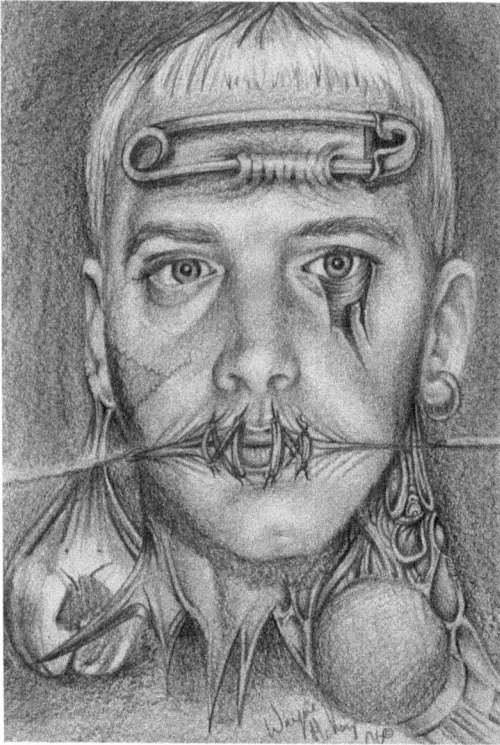

▲ *Drawing of American rapper, Eminem.*

227

Here's a rhyme:

we got kangaroos doing back flips with no pants on
look over here raw deal getting his dance on
catch me if you can im the candy man
ill jump out yah mirror and slap you sam
say my name 4 times
ill haunt you with the raw rhymes
party at my funeral put beat to the chimes
i lived hard so im slick with the flip side
getting rich quick gotta get my kids a pimped ride
who said i couldnt do it push a blade straight through it
doubt a brothers dreams now they all tried to screw it
watch me succeed with a mental twist
i got a warm bed no need to cut my wrists
evolved from the dark side rode the evil slide
had dreams of a beast now my bodys being fried
know no limits let my mind do the time
wanna get a life then i had to stop doing crime
lived the life as a silly little prangster
me and god no wanna be ganstas
thats just a taste we got all the shit that
goes on over there over here too

▲ *Me, Michele & Tahni. My little girl, the completing piece of the puzzle. I was proud as any man could be loving everything about life. I was writing my book after just being released from Ivanhoe.*

I tell people selling drugs to kids exactly what I think of them. I sing about what I would like to have done to the people who fucked me over in my life. Music is my way of getting high without drugs. When I have the mic in my hand I'm at peace with myself.

The first time I heard myself on a CD I spun out. It was a good feeling to know I could do something like that and make it sound good. A lot of people think I'm crazy but the proof is in the pudding. My songs that I create about my family and my love for them are my favourite songs. When my daughter came home from the hospital I wrote her song in a day. Some days I can write three songs. Others I can just keep writing to whatever beat is playing. All day long. I have thousands of rhymes. They are only words. Hit me with your evilest of curses, I will rhyme till I die. I got plenty of verses. If you don't like what I say, you best turn the other way. I'm here to help not here to play.

I am a man, a husband, and a dad, trying to give my family the things I never had. Twenty-seven years old I started from scratch. Twenty-nine now and I am about to hatch.

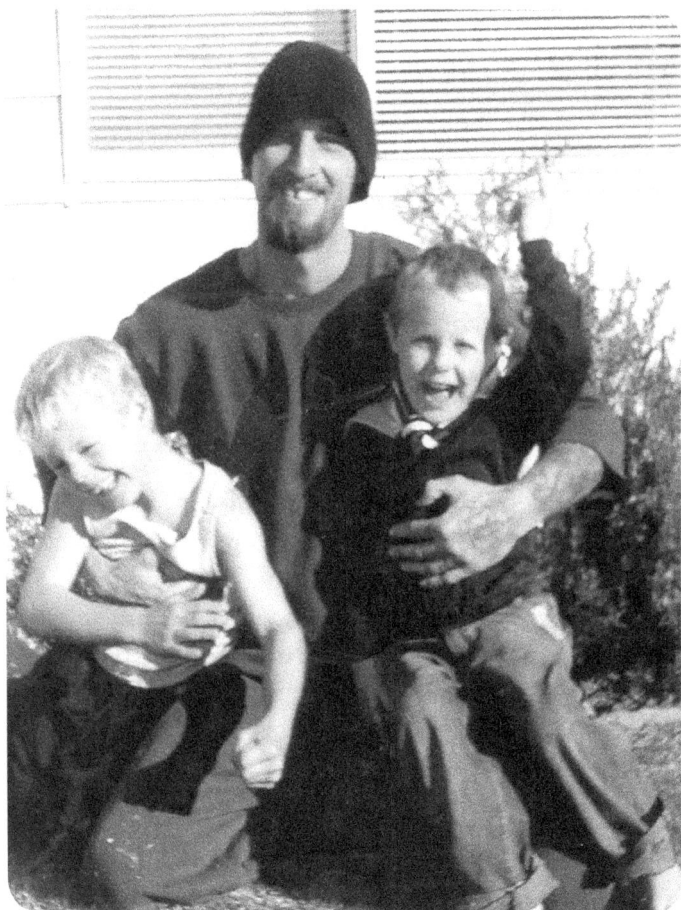

▲ *Me and my lads.*

TWO STAUNCH SONS

Dads two little soldiers
I watch you grow older
Your attitudes change
both a little bit bolder
youbothgotyourownmindsnow
thinkin about things more
whats tomorrow gonna bring
who knows whats in store
two little hard nuts now
not babys no more
i know i can be a hard man
that scares with his roar
i know im not your real dad
and that can be hard
but im doing my best
to get you both a head start
i dont tell you enough
how much i love you
but i think it all the time
ihopethisrhymewillshowyou
ryley my little sawn off
you been tuff from the start
your attitudes never worn off
with you strong little heart

youll be a leader one day
you and jayden both
two staunch little men
i pray you get the most
out off the lives you live
remembertogetyougottagive
you both light a light for me
even if you doubt it
both your hearts are in mine
and id be lost without it
youbothcangetonmynerves
i cant deny that
but every road has its curves
andidontmindthatigetonyour
nerves too
being a grumpy old prick
but remember this though
staunch i will stick
i got your backs for eva
one day youll see
thatallthethingsivesaidwasnt
just for me

Wayne Mackay

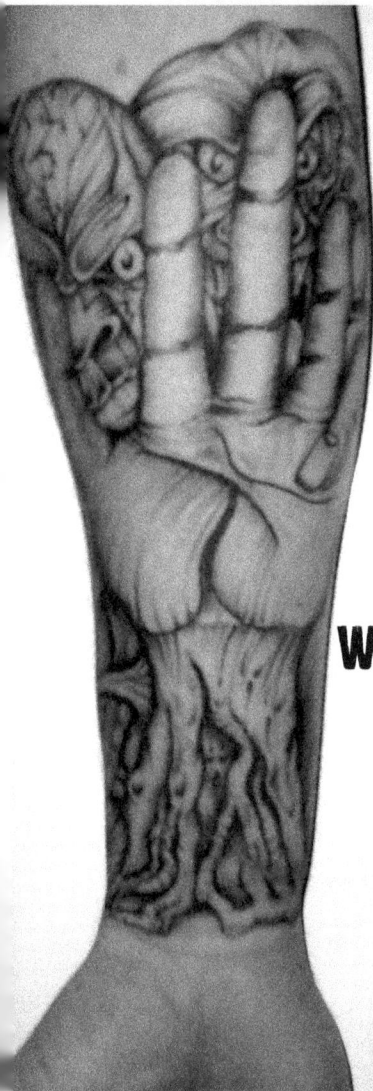

10

EPILOGUE
WHERE I AM NOW

I'm at peace with myself and I'm happy. Doing what I want to do through my music I'm helping some of the youth in Geelong who have been involved with the Torch Program. This is a program that helps underprivileged kids. Not all of them are underprivileged, some have very nice parents who themselves are volunteering to help out as well. From what I've seen the goal of the project is to bring people together in the community and see what can be done to make some changes, as well as giving the youth something to do.

I got involved with the Torch Program through one

of my partner's friends, Kahlie, who had been doing the program for a couple of weeks. She had seen the youth there doing the hip hop practices and said she knew me and what I was involved in with my music studio and so they asked me to come and see them. I hadn't been involved with anything like that before. The first time I walked into the hall where they held the program I was nervous, wondering if people would spin out on me and my personality, the way I talk, my views on things. I didn't know what I was walking into. I thought I was just going down to help some kids who were getting in trouble with the law to make a CD and that was it. There were people I'd never seen before and people I wouldn't normally associate with. Me and my family were accepted into the little group straight away. Me— all covered in tattoos and teeth missing, with the look of a nutcase—and no one had a problem with me.

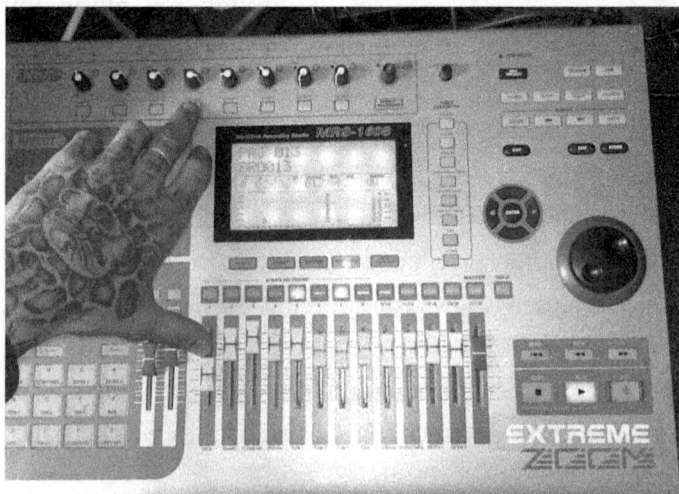

▲ *My mixing desk.*

That was where it all started for me, branching out into the community. I ended up being in a play about domestic violence and other issues that go on in the lower income areas, it also happens in the upper class living arrangements too but this was about those other suburbs: the one's where I am from (and I'm proud of it) in Western Australia. Torch also pointed out that not all people from these areas are lost causes and junkies. That shit happens all over the world: people being judged because they are different, misfortunate or struggling to get through. Sometimes people try to stay away from the lower income areas because of the crime rate and things that go on but then the people who are living there miss out on a lot of what goes on in the other areas. It looked to me like Torch was trying to change that and I wanted to be part of it.

I had never been in a play before so it was a new experience for me. Firstly, I started working with another Aussie hip hop artist Mattricks and about 8 young fellas. Mattricks had been doing a bit of work with them so they all pretty much knew what they were doing and had rhymes made up. No bullshit, I have to admit I didn't know how we were going to make it work but Mattricks is a genius at what he does and he pieced everything together. I wasn't sure what my purpose was so I just sat there whilst my son and his new mates wrote rhymes. I told them what I did when I rhymed. That I imagined the person I wanted to talk to was right there in front of my face. That whoever or whatever my rhyme was about I blocked myself off from the world around me. Some of the kids didn't know how to take me but they all got used to me I think. I haven't had as much fun as what I did with that Torch bunch in all my life.

The Whitt was the name of our show that we put on and we ended up doing two shows after about 4 months of weekly practice. We had dinner at all the rehearsal nights: pizza or a chef would come in and cook a big feed. There were people there to take care of the younger children, they played games in one of the spare rooms with a child worker. We had to sign our children in and out so we knew they were safe. I remember all the adults that were involved, although I don't remember all their names, their faces and their friendly nature. Being someone who hasn't really taken the time to get to know many people outside of my circle it opened my eyes.

I'll be honest. I didn't really like or have much time for anyone outside of my style of living. In a way I resented them because a lot of people from high class areas judge people from the lower income areas—the same as I judged them. I saw them all as snobs but what I didn't realise was all the way through the project I was working with people who were coming from all around to be involved. Two people in particular had sold their house and were just travelling around doing that. Man, I had no idea people were out there that actually gave a shit. I talked with everyone there, at least I think I did. What started out as a little group of about 12 turned into a big family of about 60. I was playing the part in the show of an abusive husband. I thought I could do that no wor-

▲ *More photos of my studio all decked out with my tattoo designs, music equipment and my paintings.*

▼ *My equipment and mixing desk.*

▲ *Me and some of the lads I've been workin' with: my little dog*
willie deal D.K., T.J., Mysteriouz, JT Handsome projects and Prophet.

ries—not that I am an abusive partner. I just have had
experience at putting a point across with a twist of ag-
gression. I'm no woman basher and I don't like people
who are but playing the part was fun. I had to argue with
Kahlie our family friend so it was all good. I liked telling
her a thing or two. My partner Michele played a few different parts as well. Michele didn't think she would be in
the play but she was and she breezed it in like a natural.
I only had a few short lines in the play and was asked to
do another short part, which involved yelling about who
got custody of the kids in an argument. About a week
before the big night I was asked if I could do a song—I
said yes before I had even thought about it properly. I
had never performed live in front of an audience like

this. I had to write and rehearse a song in a week. I asked Justin, a keyboard player from out-of-this-world who I hope to work with a lot more in the future, if he could make a certain style of beat for me and he blew me away. He came to my house and we went straight to my studio. Within half an hour he had a masterpiece for me. I knew what chorus line I was going to use but I had to dig deep for my verses. I wasn't rapping for no nighttime gangsters, I was doing it for parents, grandparents, children and many other family members. The song I used was called *Ashes to Ashes*.

Both shows were booked out. Seeing the excitement in people's faces when the big night, Saturday 7 July 2007, came around was great. Everyone had a ball. The people who did the music side of it all were unreal, Justin really did some magic on the night. All the people there were great, I can't find enough words to explain what happened that night for me and my family and I dare say many of the other families.

I had a ball doing it and a lot of people asked when I was going to bring out a CD. People came up and shook my hand saying it was unreal—I shit myself. I didn't know what to say when people wanted to talk to me so if I didn't talk to you it was because I was nervous and I had no idea how to react to a compliment.

I am proud to say I will back the Whitt community in anything they do like this.

To see the end result of all that work was a trophy in itself for everyone involved: the dedication people showed to turn up on rehearsal nights showed how much these people wanted to be heard and not judged and have a good time. I believe there should be outreach programs continuously run because these youth are all great kids, they really are, and they deserve to have every opportunity any other child out there has.

Treat people like scum and usually they start to act like it. Give them a bit of pride and watch what it does. A lot of older people want to pull their noses out of their arses as well. I respect my elders and teach people around me to as well but a lot of them don't show the youth respect. They think that because they are older it gives them the right to be automatically hard and that means they don't have to listen to a child's point of view. That's bullshit. There are still too many adults out there talking and not enough listening to what their children have to say. Everyone as a community has to pull together and support these little blokes having a go at it. These kids are the future. Let's help them find positivity again. People might say what about the things I speak of in my songs? Well, all I can say is listen to the words with an open mind. I have no doubt in the world that a number of the fellas I have been working with will go on to do great things. Not because of me but because people took the time to listen and work with them.

After the Torch Program most of us have stayed in contact. We had a catch up night: pizzas and looked at photos from the big night. It wasn't long after that me and my son Jayden were rung up and asked if we would take part in a little show for the suits that were coming to announce something. I had no idea who they were or how many of them there were going to be but we agreed to do it pretty much straightaway. Mattricks said it would be great if I could walk out and introduce the boys and sing along with them on their first track. That was no drama. We had two rehearsals and not everyone showed up but still the lads ended up recording one song and writing another one to do on the day. Them eight boys are incredibly talented and deserved every bit of publicity they got to pull off what they did on the day. It was a pleasure working with them and Mattriks. The reaction they got from the audience on the day was unreal and I spun out on how many people came up and thanked me and shook my hand. The looks on all the kids' faces were ones to remember and they all got their photos in the Advertiser and in the Geelong Independent standing near the Minister of Youth Affairs. The minister also announced that the youth in Whittington, Newcomb and Thompson would have access to $225,000 to improve their community. There is some talk of electronic story telling devises and murals and heaps of other things that they can do that is a big step forward for the community.

• • •

I have been doing what I wanted to do: that is living a normal family life trying to help others as well. I really

▲ *The 3210 boys "Whittington" when we first started*
working together (source Geelong Advertiser).

▼ *Me with all the little gangstas and Shilo my female vocalist.*
The young fellas came along way through all their work. Good on yah boys.
(source Geelong Advertiser)

Head over heels on funding for young

BRITT SMITH

YOUNG rap group 3219 Boys rhymed about a place to keep off the streets.

And after their opening performance at a State Government announcement yesterday, the boys 'from the Whit' — as they like to label themselves — got their wish, along with the keys to the coffers.

Minister for Youth Affairs James Merlino announced youth in Whittington, Newcomb and Thomson would have access to $225,000 to improve their community.

He said possible projects they may choose to fund included making a mural, organising concerts or running electronic storytelling projects.

The money is part of the Youth Foundations Victoria Program, to which the Geelong Community Enterprise — a franchise of Bendigo Bank — has contributed $105,000 over four years.

"This is about young people in their communities being engaged. It's about them making decisions about the area they live in," Mr Merlino said at the Bellarine Living and Learning Centre.

"It gives genuine opportunities for young people to get involved in the life of their community, while at the same time building their skills and networks."

break: Jayden Davis and Youth Affairs Minister rlino watch Tyson 'MC Slam' breakdancing at the Living and Learning Centre. Picture: Mark Farrugi

▲ *The lads "3219 Boys" put on a show for the Minister of Youth Affairs.*
(source Geelong Advertiser)

243

want to look into having my own fully equipped re-cording studio and finding a radio station that will give us some airtime. I've been recording a group of about six rappers who are coming along fine. They age from 15 to 20 and they all have something to say that isn't about slapping a bitch up or pimpin' a hoe or flashing their bling bling. The world is a fucked up place and our kids are witness to all the shit we put in front of them. I'm no angel but that's why I'm here doing what I'm doing and not out robbing the local shop or using drugs no more. I'll back each one of the lads and my family a hundred percent. With my music I will make a differ-ence for some people—I already am. If you want to do something you have to work at it. You can do any thing you want if you put your passion to it. I don't promise no one anything and I tell everyone I work with I'm not giving them nothing, they have to do for themselves. I will put the tools in front of them but the rest is up to them. If they want results they work for it.

A whole lot of kids out there listen to American hip hop but I say screw that shit. I love some of their music too it's what got me started but I don't copy none of their styles. I'm an Aussie and proud of it. Everyone has a right to hip hop, a lot of youth don't follow their dreams because it's programmed into their heads that that's all they are doing—dreaming. There's no way they're gonna be a star or have a nice big house and they start to believe that. The American gansta rappers out there had it all given to them on a platter, they are nothing but mumma boys trying to sing about a lifestyle they know nothing about except what the movies have shown them. There are some real gifted kids out there and that's where I come into it with what I'm going to bring to the table.

We will flood the Australian hip hop scene with raw Aussie hard core. It's about time all the world sees what lives in the Bronx's of Australia. I'm not doing this just for me, I'm bringing the whole Australian meaning of neglect to the table. I said to Mysterious, one of the lads that's been working alongside me for a while, to stop with the American accent.

"Have you ever shot an AK 47? Or for that matter, even seen one?" I said. "You are a Kiwi, be proud of that brother, tell 'em how it is where you come from. Tell about the shit you hate that's going on around you."

My little Kiwi brother didn't like being told but he listened. He went away for a week and came back swinging with lyrics that blew me and my missus mind. I was like a proud father I'm telling you. He matched my words with a song about pollution paedophilia murder politicians—and this was from a 15-year-old Maori boy! Come sit in my seat for a day and listen to what I hear and you will see why I want to do what I am doing.

I lived all the shit I did for my family. So they don't have to do it. They can kick back and make the music. I want to make enough money so I can help a few of the youths follow their dreams.

The Bendigo bank donated money to the community of Whittington. Some of it should be used on a mobile recording studio in a caravan. Have it all decked out properly so it can be taken around to the lower in-

come areas and have a CD produced every month to
see what the young ones have to say. Have competitions
for the best rhyme, the prize could be radio play for the
song. There are a whole lot of things that can be done
with music—it heals. Every body loves some kind of
music. A lot of these kids are heading for trouble but the
main cause of that is neglect. Feeling outcast, brought
up around hate for each other or the system. The only
way that is going to stop is if people get involved. Sitting
there saying *what the fuck can I do?* Or thinking *the little
things I can do won't change a thing* are the thought patterns that are causing half of the problems.

None of the people that shook my hand on the day
of the boys 3219 show knew I had written a book or
anything about me but when they seen the work me and
Mattriks had done with the boys they knew I couldn't
be that bad a bloke. The rush I got being asked if I'd
participate with all that was a rush and a half, who needs
drugs? Did I ever see myself doing this? No way. As far
as I read into my future I rotted in a cell.

All I can say is that if you want to reap the rewards
then do something to help. More parents need to get involved in their kids' lives instead of other people's parents
doing the job for them. Give youths something positive
to do and something to take pride in. If you're wondering why I feel so strongly about what I am saying it's
because I didn't have a childhood due to neglect and I
hate seeing people going through the same thing, if not
worse. I only speak of my stories in my book but there
are people whose stories make mine look like a fairytale.

I want these kids to see what's out there and make their own decisions with clear heads not mixed with shit and jumping at the first thing that comes along.

• • •

I find it hard to hold a job so I'm my own boss. I paint pictures and sell them that way I get to keep doing what I'm doing and keeping an eye out for my family. Hopefully with this book some people out there will be willing to help me with my other projects. The studio I work with is a ZOOM Multi Track recording studio MRS 1608. It is well and truly capable of producing a professional sounding CD. I don't charge the boys to record, they bring their own blank CD and that's the same one they leave with only it has their songs on it. It doesn't cost me anything, only my time. My bills are getting paid, my children are fed and clothed well.

I don't in anyway encourage not going to school, I wish I stayed at school. Also, I will say this for anyone trying to dig for dirt on me—my past was an evil circle of hate, lies, deceit, mental games and confinement. I've pulled no punches and been as honest as I can be. If you think I am in any way a threat to any of these kids I would happily talk to you personally on the matter. If the lads are ever in trouble, which does happen because some of them are in gangs, I don't get involved. I advise them to stay away from that shit, telling them the best revenge is success. If anything, I have stopped some of them from getting into that shit. I'm no dirty old man

247

like some people I've met in my life. With me, what you see is what you get. I trust very few adults. If anything was to happen to any of the lads I work with I'd be one of the first ones there for them and their families. I AM MY FAMILY'S KEEPER.

If you can dig anything out of this you're a freak.

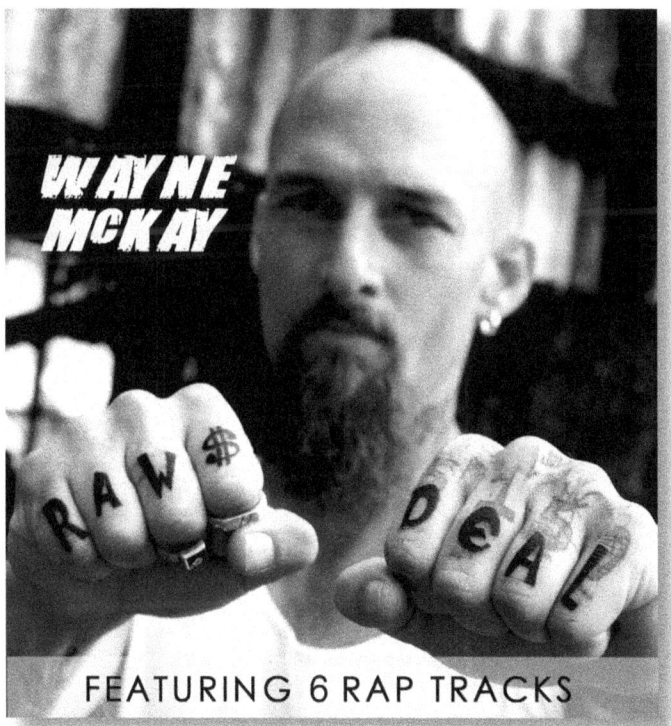

You've read about the music, now hear it for yourself.
Six original tracks by Wayne McKay coming soon from Brolga
Publishing. For order details and further information contact:
Mark Zocchi markzocchi@brolgapublishing.com.au
PO Box 12544, A'Beckett St, Victoria 8006

RAW DEAL
by Wayne McKay

ISBN 9781921221910   Qty

                    RRP   AU$24.95   .....

Postage within Australia   AU$5.00   .....

                    TOTAL* $_____

                    * All prices include GST

Name: ....

Address: ....

Phone: ....

Email Address: ....

Payment: ❏ Money Order ❏ Cheque ❏ Amex ❏ MasterCard ❏ Visa

Cardholder's Name: ....

Credit Card Number: ....

Signature: ....

Expiry Date: ....

Allow 21 days for delivery.

Payment to: Better Bookshop (ABN 14 067 257 390)
                 PO Box 12544
                 A'Beckett Street, Melbourne, 8006
                 Victoria, Australia
                 Fax: +61 3 9671 4730
                 admin@brolgapublishing.com.au

BE PUBLISHED

Publishing through a successful Australian publisher. Brolga provides:
- Editorial appraisal
- Cover design
- Typesetting
- Printing
- Author promotion
- National book trade distribution, including sales, marketing and distribution through Macmillan Australia.

For details and inquiries, contact:
Brolga Publishing Pty Ltd
PO Box 12544
A'Beckett St VIC 8006

Phone: 03 9662 2633
Fax: 03 9671 4730
bepublished@brolgapublishing.com.au
markzocchi@brolgapublishing.com.au
ABN: 46 063 962 443